# ON THE TRAIL OF LIBERATION

## VOLUME 2

*A Recounting of
Precious Moments with Amma*

Mata Amritanandamayi Center
San Ramon, California, USA

ON THE TRAIL OF LIBERATION VOLUME 2

A Recounting of Precious Moments with Amma

Edited by Br. Madhavamrita Chaitanya

Published by:
 Mata Amritanandamayi Center
 P.O. Box 613
 San Ramon, CA 94583-0613, USA
 Website: www.amma.org

Copyright © 2021 by Mata Amritanandamayi Center
All rights reserved.
No part of this publication may be stored in a retrieval system, transmitted, reproduced, transcribed or translated into any language in any form, by any means without the prior agreement and written permission of the publisher.

In India:
 www.amritapuri.org
 inform@amritapuri.org

In Europe:
 www.amma-europe.org

In US:
 www.amma.org

| 24. | Leading the World with Love  
*Br. Mokshamrita Chaitanya* | 214 |
| 25. | World Leader  
*Bri. Visvapriyamrita Chaitanya* | 226 |
| | Glossary | 231 |

# PREFACE

For her children, Amma is the center of the universe. Their thoughts revolve around her. Their words relive experiences with her. Their deeds reflect her teachings. Amma is the centripetal force drawing them ever closer to her heart—the still point of the world and a safe harbor of peace.

This book—the second volume of the compilation of *satsangs* (spiritual discourses)—begins with a message from Amma on the necessity of cultivating inner stillness. A still mind is like a diamond that can cut through the illusions of life. Forged in the smithy of *sadhana* (spiritual practice), this priceless gem is the sole currency that can procure *moksha* (spiritual liberation).

Stillness is preceded by soul-searching. Satsangs, essentially a form of *shravana* (listening), can help us introspect if our listening leads us to *manana* (contemplation) and *nididhyasana* (meditation). Each satsang in this book is a stocktaking by monastics—a reappraisal of how Amma has shaped their lives for the better; a reflection on the teachings that have aided their inner growth and flowering; and a record of gratitude, devotion and faith.

We hope that each chapter will resound like a bell, its clangor stunning the mind into a reverential hush that will eventually pave the way to total inner silence.

*Br. Madhavamrita Chaitanya*

# A STILL MIND

*A Message from Amma*

Children, the mind is a flow of thoughts. There is never a moment when the mind stops thinking. At times, the flow of traffic on the roads will be fast and furious, or, at other times, slow and leisurely. But it is not so with thoughts. Often, the flow of thoughts does not abate even in sleep. It is the mind's nature to brood over the past and to fret about the future.

Once, a middle-aged man was traveling in a train. A young man sitting beside him asked, "What's the time?"

Hearing this, the man said, "Shut up!"

Another passenger witnessing this interaction asked, "He only asked you for the time. Why do you need to get so angry over such a simple request?"

The man replied, "Yes, he asked only for the time. Suppose I tell him the time. He will start talking about the weather. He will then talk about the headlines in today's newspaper. He will talk politics next. Then he will ask about my family. I might then inquire about his family as well. Having thus become acquainted with each other, I might invite him home after disembarking. He might even spend a night there. I have a beautiful daughter, who might fall in love with him. Or he might fall in love with her. I shall never agree to my daughter marrying a man who does not even own a watch. This is why I shut him up right at the start to avoid any further conversation."

If someone asks for the time, we can either tell him the time or keep quiet. Was there any need for this man to imagine so much of the future? Because of the conflict in his mind, the other passengers also could not have peace of mind.

If the mind says 'stop' while we are walking, our legs will stop moving immediately. If the mind says 'stop' while we are clapping, the hands will stop moving at once. However, if we tell the mind to stop, will it? No. That said, we should be able to stop the mind. This is why we practice meditation. Just as we use a remote control to turn the television and other electric appliances on and off, meditation can help us bring the mind under our control.

Above all, we need a still mind to realize our true nature. We can enjoy supreme bliss and peace only in that stillness. May my children be able to awaken to such a state.

# 1

# Promise of Peace
*Br. Amoghamrita Chaitanya*

What does it mean to be a follower of Amma? It has nothing do with physically trailing her. Amma's feet represent *satya* (truth) and *dharma* (righteousness). The feet confer both stability and mobility. Amma is rooted in and moves in truth and righteousness. When we prostrate at her feet, we reverence the virtues she embodies, and strive to express those values in our life.

Similarly, being a votary of the *Bhagavad Gita* means grasping the essence of its verses, contemplating them constantly, and assimilating the teachings in our own life for the good of all. Although all the verses in the *Gita* are significant, there are a few that we must strive to remember always. Even if we cannot learn the entire *Gita* by heart, it would be worth our while memorizing at least these few. They are useful to everyone, whether or not we are seekers, for the message conveyed by these verses are universal and all-encompassing. In fact, the hallmark of the *Bhagavad Gita* is its universality.

The benedictory hymn of the *Bhagavad Gita*, traditionally recited before chanting the *Gita* verses, contains the following line:

> *amba tvam anusandadhami bhagavad gite bhava dveshinim*

> O Mother (*Bhagavad Gita*), who is the antidote to repeated births, I meditate upon you.

The term '*bhava*' is often used synonymously with '*samsara.*' Samsara is defined thus: *sam sarati iti samsara*—that which is ever changing. By meditating on (assimilating the teachings of) the *Bhagavad Gita*, we can go beyond the ever changing to the changeless substratum of the universe.

One of the most celebrated sayings in the *Bhagavad Gita* is '*kamat krodho'bhijayate,*' which means 'desire gives rise to anger.' It occurs in verse 62 of chapter 2; the following verse is also quoted here to provide a fuller picture of the context:

> *dhyayato vishayan pumsah sangas teshupajayate*
> *sangat sanjayate kamah kamat krodho'bhijayate*
> *krodhad bhavati sammohah sammohat smrti-vibhramah*
> *smrti-bhramshad buddhi-nasho buddhi-nashat pranashyati*

> Pondering on sense objects, man develops attachment to them. From attachment springs the desire to possess the objects, and desire gives rise to anger.

> From anger arises delusion, and from delusion, a bewilderment of memory. When the memory is bewildered, discriminative intelligence is destroyed. This loss of intelligence leads man to complete ruin. (2.62 – 63)

There are many objects in the world, objects that we see, hear, taste, smell and touch. When we ponder on them, we form an attachment to them. Then, the objects become the subjects of our infatuation.

For example, if A notices B passing by, B is an object of A's sight. When A looks again, she realizes that B is the man who had once teased her, causing her anguish. This recollection transforms object B into a subject in A's mind.

In the *Ashtavakra Gita*, when Sage Ashtavakra is asked about how to attain spiritual liberation, he says, "Forgo the subject (*vishayam*) if you want liberation."

Amma expresses the same idea in her own inimitable style. About three decades ago, she told me, "Son, would you drink *payasam* (sweet pudding) if you knew that it has been contaminated by lizard droppings? Look on the pleasures of this world with the same revulsion!"

Bhartrhari was once an emperor. He renounced all his wealth and went to perform austerities in a forest. One day, as he was going to bathe, his attention was drawn to something glittering. He looked and saw a precious stone lying on the ground. As he was about to pick it up, he suddenly thought, "How strong Maya (the divine power of delusion) is! I owned thousands of precious gems when I was an emperor. But didn't I renounce them all when I left for the forest? Shame on me for attempting to pick this up."

I am reminded of Amma's words: "Problems arise when there is no gap between thought and action. If there is a gap, light will fill up that gap." Another word for that light is awareness. Bhartrhari was saved from sinking again into worldliness by the benevolent light of awareness.

We would certainly do well to cultivate awareness so that it can come to our aid when we are overwhelmed by emotions like anger, sorrow and despair. We can never gratify our desires fully. Aspiring to do so is akin to pouring ghee into fire in order to put it out.

Let us return to Bhartrhari. Out of curiosity to see what would happen next, he hid behind some bushes. After some time, two brothers, who were princes, came by. One of them spotted the precious stone and showed it to his brother, who seized the gem at once. The first brother claimed that he was the rightful owner as he had seen it first. A fight broke out between the brothers, and in the clash, both died. The gem remained where it was.

Here is another example. There was a family comprising parents and three sons. The youngest son alone lived with his parents in their ancestral home. During his return home, the eldest son noticed three teak trees in the garden and began to covet them. He hoped that his father would bequeath the property to him and began fantasizing about how the timber would make him rich.

In his will, the father bequeathed the property to his youngest son. The eldest son became so upset that he began to regard his father and youngest brother as enemies and started brooding revenge on them. He lost all discretion and picked a quarrel with his younger brother. The verbal spat escalated into physical violence, culminating with the eldest brother killing his younger brother.

Both these examples illustrate the extent to which desire can bewilder the mind. Sadly, such incidents are not uncommon these days. *Kama* (desire) and *krodha* (anger) or *raga* (attachment) and *dvesha* (aversion) are two sides of a coin. Where there is raga, there is dvesha. When we see dvesha, we can be sure that it has arisen from raga. Hence, we must avoid both of them.

The next verse in the *Bhagavad Gita* explains how we can do so:

## A Recounting of Precious Moments with Amma

*raga-dvesha-viyuktais tu vishayan indriyaishcaran
atma-vashyair-vidheyatma prasadam adhigacchati*

One who is free of attachment and aversion and is able to control the mind even when coming into contact with sense objects attains divine grace. (2.64)

Here, the word that Lord Krishna uses for divine grace is *'prasadam.'* What exactly is prasad? From the verse just quoted, we can see that it is the consequence of not being ruffled by our likes and dislikes—a calm and contented mind.

All those who have received Amma's darshan know the experience of peace, if only temporarily. While we are in Amma's arms, we forget our sorrows, jealousy, anxiety, desires and the like. In those moments, there is a temporary cessation of raga and dvesha.

Just as a piece of iron is magnetized by repeated contact with a magnet, Amma's virtues tend to rub off on us. If we can repeat the moments of spiritual togetherness with Amma, we can sustain our improvement. This is Amma's real prasad.

I still remember one of Amma's injunctions: "Child, avoid unhealthy competition." The source of jealousy and greed is desire, which can be directed towards anything: money, fame or position. Instead of fixating on the objects of desire, let us try to be remain aware of how precarious our position is in the grand scheme of life. Amma says that we ought to be like a bird perched on a dry twig—so alert that it is ready to fly off when that twig snaps.

Lord Krishna says,

*prasade sarva-duhkhanam hanir asyopajayate
prasanna-cetaso hyashu buddhih paryavatishthate*

By divine grace, all sorrows are erased. The intellect of a person who is peaceful soon becomes firmly established in God. (*Bhagavad Gita*, 2.65)

This is a promise from the Lord. May it inspire us all to free ourselves of raga and dvesha. May divine bliss fill our whole being. May we all become instruments in her hands, like rays of the sun spreading the light of Amma's unconditional pure love to all.

# 2

# Queen of Hearts
*Bri. Apoorvamrita Chaitanya*

I first met Amma when I was in 4th grade. It was 1985, and my parents, elder sister and I had gone to Amritapuri. From then on, we made it a point to visit Amritapuri during all our school vacations. Thus, my sister and I grew up in the shade of Amma's love and affection. When it came to studies, Amma was very particular that we topped the class. Her grace enabled that to happen.

As a child, I often used to get headaches. We consulted many doctors but no one was able to diagnose the problem. That year, when Amma visited Chennai, my parents told her about my headaches. She blessed a piece of sandalwood and, giving it to me, told me to apply the sandal paste from it on my forehead whenever a headache came on. Most surprisingly, I had to use the sandalwood only a few times. Thereafter, the headaches left, once and for all. I still have the sandalwood piece.

During my first year in college, Amma was traveling to the US via Chennai. When I went for darshan, Amma put my head in her lap for a long time. She then said, "Daughter, after your exams this year, come and stay in the ashram and continue studying from there."

I was so stunned and overjoyed that I did not know what to say. When I moved away from the darshan line, I saw Amma continuing to gaze at me with a smile until I reached the end of the hall. That was the most unforgettable darshan I have ever had.

My parents were not ready to believe what I told them. They were convinced only after Amma confirmed it during our next visit to Amritapuri.

Amma visited Chennai for the annual Brahmasthanam Festival soon after my exams ended. I informed her that my first-year exams were over and asked when I could join the ashram. Amma said, "Come with me when I return to Amritapuri in a few days." This was also unbelievable because, within a few days of her returning to Amritapuri, Amma was leaving for her World Tour; in those days, she never allowed anyone to join the ashram while she was away. Thus, in 1993, Amma bestowed on me the blessing of being able to stay in this holy land. I completed the remaining years of my Bachelor's degree in Mathematics via distance learning.

After this, Amma asked me to do my Master's in Mathematics. I gained admission to the Kottayam district campus of the Mahatma Gandhi University. Towards the end of my first semester, just before the exams, the college authorities informed me that my Bachelor's degree was not recognized by any university in Kerala. I had to produce an eligibility certificate from the University of Madras so that I could be allowed to sit for the exams. I informed Amma, who sent my father at once to Chennai to arrange for the necessary document. Fortunately for me, owing to unforeseen circumstances, the first semester exams were postponed.

My father could not obtain the certificate. I was left with only one choice: discontinuing my Master's degree. But Amma did not agree. She asked my father to try once again. This time, when he went to Chennai, an old friend introduced him to a university official who worked in the department issuing the certificates. That officer said that the University had stopped issuing such certificates recently. However, he was able to help my father obtain special permission from the highest authority, who facilitated the issuing of the certificate. I believe that this happened only by Amma's grace. As soon as I had submitted the certificate to the college authorities, the exam dates were announced. It was as if the University had been waiting for me. Did Amma have a hand in postponing the exams?

I completed my Master's, securing the first rank. Once again, it was Amma's grace alone that enabled me to do well.

Amma might have been educated only up to fourth grade. Yet, her love and wisdom have transformed the lives of millions throughout the world. Today, the whole world is looking to Amma, the embodiment of the Supreme, for strength and guidance. She perceives the entire universe as her own Self, and showers boundless love on all. Amma is not an individual or personality; she is a wonderful phenomenon.

Amma was once asked, "You are all-knowing. That being the case, you ought to be well-versed in all languages, right?"

She answered, "All-knowing refers to knowledge of the Eternal, which is the state of the Self. The language of pure consciousness is the language of love." This is Amma's language.

In the *Bhagavad Gita*, Lord Krishna says:

*yada yada hi dharmasya glanirbhavati bharata*
*abhyutthanam-adharmasya tadatmanam srjamyaham*

O Arjuna, whenever there is a decline in righteousness and an upsurge in unrighteousness, I manifest myself. (4.7)

This is why divine leaders like Lord Rama, Lord Krishna and Amma incarnated in the world.

How is it that avatars like Amma are able to lead the whole world? They are not like an ordinary battery that discharges easily, but like an electrical transformer. They are one with the infinite power source. Amma's infinite power is her unconditional love, which overflows as compassion and self-sacrifice. This is why everyone is attracted to Amma, like iron filings to a magnet.

We have made great strides in science and technology, but we are also disintegrating mentally. Amma often says, "In today's world, both nature and human minds are in an agitated state... It might not be possible for us to change the situations around us, but if we try, we can definitely change our attitude towards these challenging situations." This is the kind of training that Amma is giving us. We must learn how to strengthen and calm our minds. This is where the need of a spiritual master arises. Amma says, "Spiritual science and material science are not two different things. Only if we lead a life based on spiritual values can we lead a successful material life."

Dr. Vijay Bhatkar, the architect of India's national initiative in supercomputing, said, "It is Amma who inspired me to undertake the building of supercomputers. She emphasizes not only the importance of the intelligence quotient (IQ) but emotional quotient (EQ) and spiritual quotient (SQ) as well."

A good leader possesses the qualities of quick thinking, fearlessness and decisiveness. In Amma, we can see the fullness of these qualities. The 2004 tsunami showcased them abundantly. Amma was giving darshan in the Kali Temple when water gushed into the ashram from the ocean. She stopped darshan immediately and left the temple to assess the situation outside. Standing in the waters, Amma swiftly made arrangements to shift all the devotees, ashram residents and villagers to the Amritapuri campus of Amrita University (across the backwaters) and to provide them with food and accommodation. Soon after, she announced a ₹100-*crore* (₹1 billion) relief-and-rehabilitation package for the affected. Amma's comprehensive plan included building homes, and providing medical aid and vocational training. Although the tsunami had adversely affected the ashram's finances, Amma was so focused on helping others that she did not even pause to consider if the ashram could afford such an expensive relief-and-rehabilitation package. Nevertheless, by the power of her *sankalpa* (divine resolve), the ashram was able to do much more than what was announced.

Amma's actions speak louder than her words. She tells the story of a minister in a kingdom who visited a village in that kingdom and saw that it was dirty. The village head had not been able to create an awareness of hygiene and cleanliness among the villagers. The next morning, the minister started cleaning the roads in the village. Seeing this, the villagers joined the minister. In no time at all, the entire village was cleaned.

Amma's ways are like that of the minister. The senior swamis have talked about how Amma was the first person to start cleaning the ashram's septic tank. Similarly, for all the seva in our ashram, Amma is at the forefront, guiding us in doing that seva properly. In her presence, seva is always a labor of love; it is a festival. This is because of the attitude of love and selflessness Amma exemplifies while doing any work. Truly, she practices what she preaches.

What sets Amma apart from other leaders is her attitude of acceptance. Most leaders try to create an organization of people with expertise and experience in a particular task. But Amma includes even the incapable. As she has said many times, she is trying to convert rusted iron into gold. All we need to do is to allow Amma to work on us. She will awaken our dormant capabilities and make us befitting instruments for that seva. Thus, by accepting us, warts and all, Amma uplifts us and makes us useful to society.

Amma often says that no one is insignificant and, therefore, we cannot reject anyone. She embraces everyone, from tiny tots to elderly people, and even animals. Not only that, everyone who has come to Amma feels that he or she is special to Amma. The Malayalam actor, Salim Kumar, recounted that when he first met Amma, he was suffering from a serious ailment. After inquiring about his health, she uttered just one sentence: "Son, Amma needs you!" This one sentence brought about a great change in his life. He gained immense mental strength and confidence, and this, in turn, helped him heal. Everyone in the world is looking for this kind of care and concern.

Once, the day after she returned from a World Tour, Amma visited the printing press. Many ashram residents rushed there. By the time I reached the press, there was a huge crowd. I could hardly see Amma; I only heard loud laughter. Upset that I could not see her, I felt that there was no point in standing there anymore. On my way back, I saw that the courtyard near the kitchen was dirty. I thought, "What if Amma returns this way?" I got a broom and started sweeping the area. After a few minutes, I felt someone patting me from behind: it was Amma. She beamed at me and lovingly said, "Daughter, you are from the city of Chennai, where there is hardly any courtyard. How then did you learn to sweep so well, like villagers?"

"I learnt to sweep only after coming here, Amma," I replied.

Amma asked the people standing near the kitchen to fetch another broom, and then started to sweep along with me. In the next few minutes, Amma and I swept the entire area near the kitchen. She then gracefully returned to her room. Through this small gesture, Amma not only dispelled my sorrow, she also made me feel recognized by praising me for an insignificant thing I had done.

One who dwells at the level of the intellect can never become a good leader. There was a smart and hard-working student. Once, when he went to sit for an exam, he became nervous when he saw the questions. Not being able to recall the answers, he lost all confidence, panicked and fainted. Seeing this, his teacher rushed to him, revived him, and whispered a few words into his ear. The boy started answering the questions.

Not only did the boy pass with flying colors, he even scored the highest mark. Later, when his friends asked him what the teacher had said, he replied, "My teacher told me, 'Child, why do you fear? Don't you know that I'm going to evaluate your answers? I know how hard you study and how intelligent you are. So, don't be scared! Just write whatever you remember; I will take care of the rest.'"

These words instilled courage and confidence in him. The teacher was able to uplift the student only because he came down to the level of the boy and understood him.

Isn't Amma like this also? At every step, she gives us courage and moral support: "Children, don't worry. Amma is with you.

Don't lose hope." She is the Universal Mother, who wants us to awaken the inner motherhood in all, both women and men.

All of us want to succeed in whatever we do. But the outcome of our efforts might not be what we desire or expect. To turn an adverse circumstance to our advantage — this is an indispensable quality for a leader, and it is one that Amma has demonstrated throughout her own life. Right from her childhood, she has faced innumerable challenges. In spite of that, Amma has overcome them all because she accepted situations as they came and adapted to them. Amma says that we should learn from ants and snakes — no matter what they encounter, they always move forward.

I am reminded of a devotee named Purnima, who is wheelchair bound. On darshan days, we can see her distributing tokens. On other days, she goes to the ashram hospital to prepare slips of paper for patients. She tries to participate in all the ashram activities, including darshan, meditation and bhajans. I once saw the following scene: a small cart containing the freshly washed laundry of visitors was attached to Purnima's wheelchair by a string, and she was steering her wheelchair to the flats where the laundry would be hung out to dry. The sight so moved me that tears welled up in my eyes. Notwithstanding the fact that her life is filled with challenges, Purnima is ever trying to serve her community through acts of selflessness.

What inspires Purnima? Amma's life and teachings. Every single individual can learn from Amma's life. In fact, her life is her message.

Amma has often said, "Don't think about what you can take; instead, always try to think about what you can give." When the then President of India, Dr. A.P.J. Abdul Kalam, came to Amritapuri to inaugurate the Amrita Setu bridge, he said, "Whenever I come to Amritapuri, the message I receive is that of giving; go on giving." Amma's life is an eloquent and ongoing expression of this very message.

In the *Bhagavad Gita*, Lord Krishna says:

> *tasmat tvam uttishtha yasho labhasva*
> *jitva shatrun bhunkshva rajyam samrddham*
> *mayaivaite nihatah purvam eva*
> *nimitta-matram bhava savya-sacin*
>
> Therefore, arise and acquire glory. Conquer your enemies and enjoy a prosperous kingdom. They have already been killed by me. O Arjuna, just be an instrument. (11.33)

We can see Lord Krishna ready to give credit for his feats to Arjuna. Likewise, whenever asked about her accomplishments, Amma says, "My children do everything. They are my wealth." Although she alone inspires and guides us, she takes no credit and makes no claims either.

Amma guides her children from different walks of life, based on their differing levels of understanding. Many years ago, Amma addressed a group of scientists in Mumbai, who wanted to ask her some questions. After answering their queries, she asked them, "What is more expansive than outer space?" None of the scientists could answer her question. Finally, Amma smiled and said, "The inner world. What have we done to explore the mysteries of the inner world?" The scientists were dumbstruck by Amma's profound words.

Amma has received many recognitions and awards for her various accomplishments. At all these functions, she accepts these awards in one of two ways: Amma either bows down to the memento, which is then collected by someone near Amma; or she receives it with all humility, and proffers it to her children to indicate that it belongs to them. Amma is able to do this because she is selfless and humble, and not attached to the results of her actions.

When we say that a man is managing 100 people, what is he actually doing? He is managing 100 minds. The larger the group, the more efficient and capable the leader ought to be. Amma has a following of millions, whom she is guiding. We can only imagine what a powerful leader she must be.

For most leaders, their leadership is restricted to a limited domain because their understanding and knowledge are limited. But Amma, whose heart is so expansive as to transcend barriers such as caste, creed, nationality and language, is extending her leadership to people throughout the world. Amma is a true world leader of this age.

# 3

# Wondrous
*Br. Sachinmayamrita Chaitanya*

*ashcaryavatpashyati kashcidenam ashcaryavadvadati canyah ashcaryavaccainamanyah shrnoti shrutvapyenam veda na caiva kashcit*

Some see the Self as wondrous. Some describe it as wondrous. Some hear of it as wondrous. Others, even on hearing, cannot understand it at all. (*Bhagavad Gita*, 2.29)

This spiritual teaching is astonishing, marvelous, a miracle. The reality of the *atma*—the all-pervading Self—is a wonder.

This verse appears close to the beginning of Lord Krishna's teaching. Standing between the two great armies, Arjuna has fallen into utter despair. Looking at the army he must fight, he breaks down and tells Lord Krishna that he does not want to fight. While Arjuna detests some in the opposing army, knowing them to be wicked, he adores some of them—specifically Drona and Bhishma. To fight means to harm them, maybe even to kill them, and so, never to see them again. This is too much for Arjuna to bear. He seeks Lord Krishna's advice, supplicating him as a disciple, and admitting his ignorance and total confusion. He asks the Lord if he should fight or not.

Krishna understands that Arjuna's problem does not arise from a lack of clarity regarding the *dharma* (duty) of a soldier. Arjuna knows that dharma through and through. His confusion, rather, is centered on his crippling attachment to certain members of the enemy army. So, even though Arjuna has ostensibly asked, "Which is for the best—to fight or to run away?" Lord Krishna decides to go to the root of Arjuna's confusion and answer him at a much deeper level.

Lord Krishna knows the crux of Arjuna's confusion is a lack of clarity regarding his own nature: he simply does not understand who he is and who the others are. Hence, Lord Krishna begins teaching Arjuna *atma-vidya*, knowledge of the Self—what is the soul? What is its relationship with this phenomenal world?

When Lord Krishna begins this teaching, he doesn't tread lightly. He tells Arjuna that crying over the deaths of Bhishma and Drona is ridiculous because they are not the body or mind but the Self. As such, they can never be hurt and they can never die. Even if Arjuna kills them, they still won't die. As the Self, they have always existed and will never cease to be. This isn't just the case for Bhishma and Drona, but for all beings. Krishna explains to Arjuna that we are nothing but pure consciousness, passively observing all the changing stages of life: infancy, youth, middle age, old age, even birth and death. Not only is the Self indestructible, Lord Krishna says it is also all-pervading, transcending time and space. Moreover, even if Arjuna fights, the real Arjuna will not fight, for the Self is eternally action-less.

In essence, Krishna says, "We are all the one birthless, eternal, unchanging, omnipresent consciousness upon which this ephemeral creation hovers like a dream. So, Arjuna, don't worry.

Don't feel sad about having to fight and kill Drona and Bhishma because it's not that big a deal."

Arjuna cannot believe what Krishna has told him. It's just too astonishing. At the same time, the little bit he has understood has completely blown his mind.

Why is this teaching so wondrous? It is partly because our understanding of our self, the world and God is totally wrong! We think we are mortal, but the Guru tells us we are immortal. We think we are finite, fixed in one time and space, but the Guru says that we pervade the entire cosmos and that we do not move through time; rather, time moves through us. We think happiness comes from fulfilling our desires, but the Guru says that we are the source of bliss. We think we are separate from other beings in the world, but the Guru says that our self is the very self of all beings. We think we are born into this world and disappear from it when we die, but the Guru says that the world is born in us, and that we are the one permanent reality from which all changing names and forms arise.

Adi Shankaracarya and subsequent commentators say that the word *ashcaryavat* need not refer only to how the Self is seen, spoken about and heard of, but also refer to the subjects of those sentences. One who sees, speaks and hears is a wonder, too.

To me, we all are wonders. I don't mean that we are saints. But the fact that I am here with Amma—that, at least to me, is a wonder. Because if I look back at who I was before meeting Amma—my attitudes, desires, goals and ignorance—then, the fact that I am here now is nothing short of a miracle, because I was not spiritual at all.

My cousin first met Amma. Around 1996, he became interested in spirituality. Seeing the transformation in his personality, I thought he had gone insane. But after a while, I realized that he had just given up bad habits that I thought were part and parcel of life. He was calmer and happier. When we met, he would talk about spirituality sometimes, and I would half listen.

One day, I was flipping through his scrapbook, which had photographs of various saints and gurus. With long beards, shaved heads and dreadlocks, many of them looked like they came from a different solar system! Suddenly, I noticed a photo of a tiny, round lady, with her hair in a bun and a mischievous smile. "Who's that?" I asked.

He told me it was Amma, and that people wait in line for hours and hours to get a hug from her. A faint voice within me said, "I want a hug."

"Do you want the photo?" he asked.

"Sure, yeah, okay."

It was a small, black-and-white, passport-sized photo. I stuck it in the bottom left corner of my bedroom mirror, between the wood frame and the glass. After that, every day, Amma would be there, smiling at me as I got ready for work. I remember looking down at that photo and being bemused by that smile. Why was she smiling?

I've heard it said that just seeing a photo of a *mahatma* (spiritually illumined being) initiates a spiritual awakening. When a tiny ray of sunlight touches a seedling, it begins to unfurl gradually. The rest of my life unfolded from seeing that photo. What started out as a small ray of love finding its way to me, soon expanded. Less than a year later, I was in Amma's San Ramon ashram, waiting in line for darshan. Being in Amma's arms was like being hugged by the sun itself.

## A Recounting of Precious Moments with Amma

How did I get to Amritapuri just two short years after meeting Amma and began this life with a mind that was so undisciplined, attached and confused? That can be nothing but wondrous grace.

Not that it was easy. The transition was, in fact, quite difficult and, at times, very painful. When you've been holding on to thorns for so long, even letting go spills a lot of blood.

I remember reading one of Amma's books not long after meeting Amma. I was in bed, the desk lamp was on, and I read the following story. Two astrologers, who were close friends, were curious to know about their next births, and did some calculations. One discovered he would be born as an elephant; the other, as an earthworm. The one who was destined to be an earthworm became depressed. He told his friend, "Promise me that in your next life, you will search for me. When you find me, just crush me with your foot. Hopefully, I can be reborn with a body of merit."

His friend solemnly promised.

Eventually, they both died. As foretold, one was born as an elephant and the other as an earthworm. But whereas the elephant-astrologer remembered their past lives and the promise, the earthworm-astrologer had completely forgotten. The elephant-astrologer began searching for his old friend. One day, he lifted a rock and—low and behold—there he was, wiggling around in the dirt with several other worms. The elephant-astrologer quickly raised his foot to crush him. But when he did so, the tiny voice of the worm-astrologer cried out, "Stop! What are you doing? Are you insane? You've just destroyed my beautiful house! Go away! Don't kill me! Leave me alone!"

I don't think I slept that night. It was as if Amma had lifted the rock under which I was hiding and showed me how utterly pointless my life was—how base and selfish my goals and dreams were. The choice was mine: she would either gently place the rock back down and I could go on living in the dark or, if I was willing, I could try to lead another type of life with a different goal.

A few months later, I was on a flight to India.

Please do not misunderstand the story. It is not a comment on family life but about how narrow our perspective can be, and how our love needs to expand beyond the limited confines of 'I' and 'mine.' That can definitely be done within a family. Amma has a lot of respect for the *grhastha* (householder) dharma and so do I. Many of the householder devotees I have met are deeply spiritual, much more disciplined and devoted than I am. Their ability to manage both the spiritual and the material worlds, or rather, to spiritualize their material life and maintain focus on God amidst all their duties and relationships is nothing short of a wonder.

That said, I don't think that type of focus would have been possible for me. And at that stage in my life—in my late 20s, when I might have begun married life—that story about the worm was what I needed to hear.

So, when Lord Krishna says that the one who listens to atma-vidya is like a wonder, I know that to be true, not because of any greatness in me, but because I know from where I have come.

Of course, the real wonder is the one who perceives the Self and can teach about it: a *Brahma-nishtha* Guru, the spiritual master who is established in the Supreme, someone like Amma.

To know the Self is to completely understand one's own nature and to have assimilated that understanding so thoroughly that it completely pervades your subconscious. Its reality pulses in every heartbeat and every breath. A *jnani* (knower of the Self) realizes that this world of matter—the earth, wind, stars, our own body and mind, and those of all beings in creation—has arisen from himself or herself and that he or she is the very essence of all beings. When we see the world in this way, how else can we think of others but as our own darling children?

The miracle we are all experiencing in Amma—the miracle that this unobjectifiable knowledge can take a form of flesh and blood, not even five feet tall, and walk and talk and move among us—that is the Wonder of wonders.

While preparing this talk, I remembered something that happened long back when Amma was in Seattle. During a question-and-answer session, a devotee told Amma how beautiful she thought Amma's eyes were. She said, "Amma, when I look into your eyes, I feel that I can see the entire universe in them." She then asked Amma why her eyes were so beautiful and, more pointedly, if Amma had ever contemplated the beauty of her own eyes.

The depths of Amma's answer were fathomless. She said, "Amma sees her own eyes through the eyes of her children."

This is the wonder that is the jnani. We can spend hours watching Amma, listening to her, and gazing into her eyes. We can do this because we recognize—at least to some degree—how precious and rare Amma is. But for Amma, it's not just a mahatma who is wondrous. For her, everything is a wonder. She sees the same mystic beauty that we see in Amma's eyes, in all eyes. That is why Amma delights in everything: people, animals, nature, drawings by little children... She sees everything being pervaded with the infinite mystery that is the Self. This is why we find Amma so infinitely attractive and wondrous. What we find so beautiful about Amma is not really something we see, but something Amma sees.

For Amma, divinity is everywhere. The real wonder for her must be that we do not see it. Yet Amma knows that our poor vision is human nature. Until we purify ourselves of our negativities, we will continue being blind to the Self. Therefore, much more of a wonder to Amma must be our lack of effort in removing those negativities.

The scriptures declare that a human birth, association with a mahatma, and a longing for spiritual liberation are hard to come by. We have been blessed with two of these three precious boons. The third boon—the intense thirst to know and pursue the Truth—is not something God bestows. It's a boon we must give ourselves.

Amma is always reminding us how fast the sand in the hourglass of life is trickling down. In the *Mahabharata*, Yudhishthira encounters a *yaksha* (celestial being) who asks him, "What is most wondrous?"

Yudhishthira answers, "Day after day, the creatures here go to the House of Death, yet those who remain think their stay is permanent. What can be a greater wonder than that?"

I would like to offer a prayer to Amma: may we always manifest the sense of wonder we had when we first met Amma and first came to the spiritual path; may we all remember how precious this association with Amma is and do everything we can to benefit from it. If we can make that resolve and try just a little bit, then I know Amma's grace will make our efforts complete.

While everything about Amma and her knowledge is a wonder, probably the most wondrous thing about Amma is how she translates this knowledge into action. The extent to which she radiates that teaching through her every thought, word and deed is all but unprecedented in the history of spirituality. As a Guru,

Amma's emphasis has always been on *nishtha* (abidance), not just *jnana* (knowledge). Without nishtha, jnana has only limited value. For Amma, the signs of jnana-nishtha are *samatva* (equanimity) and *karunya* (compassion).

Does the knowledge that we are not the body or mind translate into even-mindedness in success and failure, praise and criticism? Does our knowledge of our oneness with all beings translate into kindness and compassion towards them? This is what Amma calls practical spirituality, and I feel it is the central message of her life.

Unlike ordinary *jivas* (individual souls), an Avatar chooses the circumstances of life: where she will be born, where she will live, what she will do...

Before this birth, Devi, the Goddess, was seated in the heavens, and she began to contemplate life on earth. She asked her *shaktis* (personifications of various divine powers), "Where should I be born?"

Perhaps thinking of a nice vacation with her, they said, "Kerala! It's so beautiful. It's God's Own Country!"

Devi said, *"Tad astu"* ("So be it"). She then asked, "To whom should I be born?"

After some thought, the shaktis said, "There is a virtuous and pious couple who live in the peninsula between the backwaters and the Arabian Sea."

"Tad astu." Then Devi asked, "But what shall I do there?"

"You can instruct people in dharma and teach them their divine nature."

"Tad astu," said Devi. "But how should I teach them that?"

The shaktis fell silent. For the ability to speak about that truth—which is beyond words and the mind, and which can never even be objectified—is a wonder. Eventually, one of the shaktis joked, "Well, maybe you can just hug them!"

The other shaktis were confused. "Hug them?"

The comedian shakti laughed and said, "Yeah, you know, like *jivatma-paramatma aikyam*," referring to the union of the individual soul and supreme soul.

Though it was meant to be a joke, Devi's eyes lit up. "Yes! I will hug them."

Seeing the look in her eyes, the shaktis became a little nervous.

Devi said, "At first, a few people will come to me. I will listen to their problems, wipe away their tears, hug them and do everything I can for them. From this, people will see what selfless and unconditional love is. Soon, there will be many, many more. I will show them what true compassion is."

The shaktis were getting more nervous. They didn't like the sound of this at all. But Devi was getting more and more excited. "And then there will be thousands, and I will hug them and shower them also with love and compassion. People will wonder, 'How can she do that for so many hours? She's not stopping to rest! Her whole life is being given over to wiping away the tears of people and consoling them! How can she tolerate it? How does she keep smiling?'

"But I will not stop. The thousands will turn into millions. Some of them will throw flowers, and some of them will throw stones, but I will love them all the same. I will show every single one the compassion they are so desperately seeking.

"Then tens of millions will come. People will say, 'Her body must be breaking!' It will, but I will still be smiling. I will show the entire world what divine love is."

The shaktis said, "O Devi, please don't do that! Do you know how painful it will be? People are ignorant. They will just want more and more from you. With their problems, questions and letters, they will never let you rest. And in spite of your teaching them and showing them the truth, the majority won't even understand! We can't even bear to think of it!"

But even as they were saying this, the bright red of Devi's sari was already starting to fade to white. Her long-flowing black hair was beginning to gather itself into a bun. And then, before their eyes, Devi's slender body began to become just a little plump and perfect for hugging.

She heard the shaktis say, "Oh Devi, this idea you have is too much for us to bear—too wondrous. Please, don't do it!"

Devi said, "No, it's perfect. That's exactly how I want it to be."

# 4

# Sacred Memories
*Swamini Sreecharanamrita Prana*

I first met Amma in 1981. I was six or seven years old. My family heard about and met Amma during a distressing period in our lives. My grandmother's hand had become paralyzed after a wooden beam fell on it. Medical treatment had failed to restore mobility in the hand. But just one gentle and compassionate stroke from Amma healed it completely. This incident convinced all of us that Amma was Divine.

Soon after that, I started visiting the ashram with my father, Ayyappan-acchan. Amritapuri has always been for me the perfect place for a spiritual retreat because of its tranquil environment. No crowd can disturb this tranquility. On days when there was no darshan, the silence would be punctuated by the rustling of leaves. If devotees visited, Amma would talk to them. The first brahmacharis (now the senior swamis) would hardly be seen. Occasionally, we would see them washing their plates after meals or gazing at Amma from afar as she spoke to devotees. I never even saw them talking to each other. If, by chance, we passed their rooms, we would see them immersed in meditation.

As a child, I did not know anything about ashrams or Gurus. For me, the ashram was like my own home. This feeling gave me total freedom to go anywhere in the ashram, even to Amma's room. I was always trailing behind her. On days when there was no darshan, I would spend almost the whole day with Amma, trailing her like a shadow as she milked the cows, ate or even lay down to rest. I received many opportunities to hold her towel, bring her water, and massage her feet. Sometimes, she would lie on a mat, laying her head on my lap. I cherish these memories as the most precious treasures of my heart.

Sometimes, our family would reach the ashram during the bhajans. Even though there were no microphones, we would hear the bhajans from across the backwaters. Maybe it was because there were no big buildings in the ashram at that time. Then as now, Amma would sing in ecstasy, forgetting her surroundings. Looking at her, our minds would also become still. After the bhajans, Amma would remain in a state of divine ecstasy for hours.

In those days, bhava darshan was held three times a week. Amma would dance at the end of Krishna Bhava and at the start of Devi Bhava. She would dance with eyes shut, expressing *mudras* in her raised hands, smiling splendidly, and dancing with one leg raised. Amma would dance at lightning speed, and yet, she never stumbled or knocked on anything, even with eyes shut. For Amma, whose inner eye is ever open, what difference does it make if her outer eyes are closed? Those scenes of her divine dance *lilas* remain indelibly etched in my memory.

After Krishna Bhava, the doors to the kalari would open after half an hour, when Amma worshipped the crown she wore during Devi Bhava. After this, Amma's father, Sugunanandan-acchan, would sprinkle holy water around the kalari. When the doors reopened, Amma would jump out with such powerful ferociousness, wielding sword and trident in her hands, that no one would dare to go near her. She would dance ecstatically while swirling.

As she danced, Amma would laugh in divine ecstasy in a way that reminded me of Goddess Kali. The brahmacharis would be singing bhajans. After dancing in one spot for a while, Amma would rush eastwards. Amma's older sister, Kasturi-amma, told me that this was where Amma had once blissfully trampled the thorns that her opponents had strewn on the ground, as if they were soft flowers. Before returning into the kalari, Amma had used her sword to shatter the glass frame of a photo and danced ecstatically on the glass pieces. Her opponents thus witnessed Kali's divine invincibility.

As she danced, Amma would move towards the devotees standing near the Mehndi (Henna) tree outside the kalari. She would bless them by touching them with her sword, which would be vibrating, just like the rest of her body. Amma would then go behind the kalari. Later, we learnt that she would bathe Dattan, the leper, there, with many pots of water, at the very end of Devi Bhava. Amma would then emerge from behind the kalari with a huge roar.

Looking back, I feel that Amma's divine dance can be compared only to the *Shiva-tandava*, Lord Shiva's divine dance. It was as if Amma was removing a veil or two, revealing glimpses of her supreme energy.

Devotees had many experiences and beliefs associated with Amma's dance. They believed that if Amma stopped in front of a person and roared in ecstatic laughter, much of his or her *prarabdha* (karmic burden) would be removed. When my mother, Kanthi-amma, heard this, she wanted to be blessed in a similar way. The very next moment, Amma came right in front of her and satisfied her wish. But seeing Amma's fearsome form and hearing her boisterous laughter, Kanthi-amma tripped and fell backwards! Luckily, there was a sand pile right behind her and she was not hurt.

An elderly devotee, Bhargavan-acchan, used to ring the bell in the kalari while Amma danced. Once, the bell suddenly stopped ringing. Not knowing what had happened, he looked at the bell and saw that the rope tied to the bell had been severed... by Amma's sword! From this, we can infer how sharp the sword was and how swift Amma's unearthly dance.

Soon afterwards, the *arati* (worship with lamps) would take place. I have had the blessing of holding the *alavattam* and *venchamaram* (ornamental fans) then.

Once, Amma came to our ancestral home after a Thursday darshan. She stayed with us for the next two days and left on Sunday morning. Needless to say, those three days were heavenly for us! We spent every moment with Amma. She played *kabaddi* (a contact team sport) with us.

At the end of the three-day stay, Amma took photographs with our entire family in groups. In those days, 'Sreekumar-*annan*' (now Swami Purnamritananda) was responsible for taking photographs in the ashram. I often heard Amma scolding him for taking more than one photograph, saying that taking too many photos will affect the 'energy' of a person. Amma has nothing to lose; it is only for our benefit that she cautions us. But on that day, she patiently stood with us, as one among the family! As mentioned before, we were a big family—grandparents, my parents and their children, Ayyappan uncle and family... I had never seen Amma pose for so many photos in those days. How many wonderful opportunities Amma gave us to be with her! Her love for her children is immense indeed.

Another precious memory is the trip to Kanyakumari with her. Amma was accompanied by the brahmacharis and a few other devotees, and we all filled a van. As we climbed Maruthva Mountain, Amma made us call out the names of Hanuman—Anjaneya, Veera, Hanumanta… Before we left, Amma went to a few shops, just like an ordinary person, to buy gifts for devotees who could not go on the trip.

In those days, Amma used to wear a long skirt and half-sari. We wanted her to wear a full sari. We took her to my grandfather's shop to buy the sari, but Amma chose to stay inside the car with us children. By the time we returned home, it was around 5 p.m. We helped Amma put on the sari. The moment we finished dressing her up, we heard the *pancavadyam* (ceremonial playing of five instruments) from the nearby temple. We were stunned! Usually, the drums were played only during the arati, which is at 6:30 p.m. Through we had been staying in that house for almost eight years, we had never once heard it being played so early. The moment the drums started playing, Amma's face took on the same expression she wears in Devi Bhava. The dressing up of Devi must be marked by fanfare, mustn't it? In my young mind, I had imagined that Amma was Devi only during Devi Bhava and 'our Amma' at other times. In that moment, was she showing us all that she was Devi Herself?

I remember another such attempt by Amma to help me understand that she and Devi are one. Once when we visited the ashram, we found Amma resting in the kalari. There was no one else there. We made her lie in our lap and asked Amma to sing a bhajan for us all. Amma sang *'Ananda Veethiyil.'* Later, while conversing with us, she said that something strange had happened a few days before. She had heard an 'mmm' sound. She looked around to find the source of the sound. After some time, she realized that it was coming from within her. Then, two powerful fangs emerged from either side of her mouth.

As Amma narrated this incident, we were all dumbstruck by awe. We ought to have understood then that Amma is Goddess Kali Herself, that the Amma in white sari is the same being as the Amma in Devi Bhava. Sadly, I did not. In my narrow understanding, Devi came when Amma called her and left after that. It took me years to understand what Amma intended through her narration.

From our experiences with Amma, we might gain the limited understanding that she is different. However, we lack the wisdom to fathom the depth of her being. We know that Amma used to give Krishna Bhava darshans and that she still gives Devi Bhava darshans; that she often says, *"Om namah shivaya;"* that the idol in the ashram's temple is that of Dakshineshwar Kali; that Amma has consecrated numerous Brahmasthanam temples... From just these few pieces of the puzzle, we might wonder, "Who is Amma?" Once, while mulling over this question, I heard that someone had asked another spiritual leader the same question and that he had said, "She is the incarnation of the Kali whom Sri Ramakrishna Paramahamsa and Sri Sarada Devi worshipped!" Perhaps, that is why Amma consecrated the idol of Dakshineshwar Kali in Amritapuri. How blessed we are to have Goddess Kali as our Guru and Mother!

Many years ago, Bri. Bindu and I had an opportunity to present a dance on Amma's birthday. As we were getting ready, we realized that we had forgotten to bring anklets for Bindu. We sat in the dressing room, wondering what to do. To our great surprise, Amma sent her own anklets, the ones she wore during

Devi Bhava! Bindu was thus blessed to wear Amma's anklets because of her innocent devotion and dedication to Amma. When Amma sees that her children need something, she willingly gives away her personal belongings. For her, the needs of her children are of prime importance.

Amma is ready to forgive all our mistakes but she will not tolerate our ego. Once, when I was 10 or 11 years old, I was sitting near Amma in the hut. There were only five or six people there, listening to Amma's words and clearing their doubts. When the topic moved to that of fear, I childishly bragged that I was not scared of *anything* as Amma was always with me! After a few moments, we noticed a snake hanging from the roof of the hut. I screamed and ran out of the hut. So much for my fearlessness!

Some of my precious memories are from Amma's Indian Tours. During one South Indian Tour, we stopped by the Bhavani River. It was here that Amma taught many of the ashram residents how to swim, by making us place our hands on her shoulders. She then washed our faces with soap, made us stand in a circle, and chant the *Lalita Sahasranama*, the 1,000 names of the Divine Mother. Amma then asked us to call out, "Amma! Amma!" and repeatedly submerge our heads in water, and showed us how. After spending time with the brahmacharinis, Amma moved to the brahmacharis and repeated the whole process with them. She spent more than five hours in the river to make us happy. Even celestial beings would have envied us!

During one North Indian tour, we stopped at the Narmada River. When we saw Amma wading into the river, we started following her. Turning around, she warned us to be careful. "Children, let Amma check the depth of the river first. Remain in the shallow waters and come only if Amma calls you."

Amma then waded into the river with a few Westerners who were expert swimmers. Seeing Amma swimming in the river, we forgot her instructions and started moving towards her. All of a sudden, we slipped into a deep pit. As I was drowning, someone caught hold of my hair firmly and lifted my head above the water. It was Amma! I felt blissful. Amma told a Western woman to take care of me and then went to rescue others.

Later, Amma compared the Narmada to an *asura* (demon) who had tried to kidnap her children. I have no doubt that if Amma had not been with us, many of us would have drowned.

At the next tea stop, I got a chance to sit near Amma. After meditation, she looked straight into my eyes and asked in a serious tone, "Do you know who saved you from drowning?" I wanted to say, "Amma, you saved me. You gave my life back to me so that I could continue living with you." But I was so choked up with emotion that I could not utter a single word. Many are the occasions when Amma rescues us, teaches us and saves us. How can we truly thank her? I pray to Amma to give me the strength to offer my life at her feet.

By Amma's grace, I started staying permanently in Amritapuri in 1991. Initially, I had many grievances—Amma was not talking as much to me as she was to others; she was not expressing love to me… Soon after that, she sent some of us to branch ashrams. Though I was sad about this, I reluctantly obeyed Amma. My mind began questioning, "Why is it that only we are being sent out? There are so many others who could have been sent instead. Perhaps, Amma doesn't love me. She doesn't want me close to her." I wrote many letters to Amma, expressing my sorrow.

Over time, Amma helped me understand that each person has his or her own karma (destiny). She gives us a particular seva after considering our character and karma. Amma helps us evolve by putting us in situations that make us confront our *vasanas* (latent tendencies), thereby helping us face them squarely. Such invaluable opportunities help us understand what Amma is trying to teach us. If we fail to understand that she is acting only in our best interests, we will be miserable. I now see the mistakes in my viewpoint, but it took me years.

When we sincerely do the seva that Amma assigns us, we will receive *punya* (merit) and attain mental purity. We will also feel a sense of personal satisfaction. Sometimes, we might think, "Who will do this seva if I'm not here?" This is the voice of our ego. Actually, seva is an opportunity that Amma has compassionately given us to exhaust our karma and gain mental purity.

The first monastics in the ashram, now the senior swamis and swaminis, did all the seva in the ashram, meditated eight hours every day, and chanted their mantra a specific number of times daily. They never complained that they had too much work to do. They are our role models. Amma never asked succeeding monastics to meditate for so long because she knew that they would not be able to withstand such severe austerities. Instead, she offered them more seva opportunities. If we do not engage our minds in seva, our mind will lead us astray. Let us not forget that the seva we do is only for our own evolution. As Lord Krishna says in the *Bhagavad Gita*:

> *ye me matam-idam nityam-anutishthanti manavah*
> *shraddhavanto'nasuyanto mucchyante te'pi karmabhih*

> Those who follow my teachings constantly, faithfully and without complaining will be released from the bondage of karma. (3.31)

Though Amma has nothing to gain, she is ever engaged in serving others. No one can do even a fraction of the work she does. Not only that, her workload has been increasing over the years. She has to help resolve the problems of her children, and she has millions of devotees all over the world. In addition, she has to oversee the running of the numerous ashram institutions and branches. Over and above all of it, Amma is engaged in uplifting the dharmic consciousness of humanity.

In the *Srimad Bhagavatam*, Yudhishthira tells Lord Yama, the god of death:

> *ahanyahani bhutani gacchantiha yamalayam*
> *sheshah sthavaram icchanti kim ashcaryam atah param*

> Day after day, countless people die, and yet those who are alive consider themselves beyond the pale of death and do not prepare for it. What could be more curious than this? (7.2.57)

To me, there is something even more baffling. Though we have all tasted Amma's unconditional love and compassion, though we know firsthand how she has transformed lives, and though we have witnessed Amma's stupendous multi-tasking abilities, are we really aware of who Amma is? In all honesty, I can say that the awareness has not sunk in yet. If we truly understand, we will have no complaints, anger or worries.

May we all be grateful for the innumerable moments of joy that Amma bestowed on each one of us. May she shower her choicest blessings on us all.

# 5

# Brahmarpanam
*Bri. Jneyamrita Chaitanya*

We cannot stare at the blazing sun with our naked eyes without risking damage to our eyes or even blindness, though we can easily gaze at the moonlight. Similarly, ordinary people cannot directly realize *nirguna* Brahman, the Supreme unconditioned by attributes. However, for our sake, the Supreme has incarnated as the Divine Mother. She is leading us by hand along the path to immortality by helping us turn our *karma* (actions) into *yajna* (sacrifice).

In the *Bhagavad Gita*, Lord Krishna talks about *Brahma-yajna*, the sacrifice of the Supreme to the Supreme. The verse has come to be known as the *Brahmarpanam mantra*, and it is traditionally chanted before every meal. Amma herself leads the ashram residents in chanting this mantra every Tuesday after she has distributed lunch to all.

> *brahmarpanam brahmahavir brahmagnau brahmanahutam*
> *brahmaiva tena gantavyam brahma-karma-samadhina*

> Brahman is the ritual sacrifice. Brahman is the oblation (sacred offering), which is offered by Brahman to the fire of Brahman. One who sees Brahman in everything attains Brahman. (4.24)

This mantra contains the essence of Vedanta because it illustrates the scriptural dictum, *"Sarvam khalvidam brahma"*—"This whole universe is Brahman indeed" (*Chandogyopanishad*, 3.14.1.). In the previous verse of the *Bhagavad Gita*, Lord Krishna says that the actions of a *jnani* (knower of Brahman), who always acts in a spirit of yajna, do not leave any impression on his mind because he acts with detachment. Actions and their results do not bind a jnani, who is like butter floating on water—ever detached from the surroundings. Such actions are known as Brahma-karma. Brahman is both the way and the goal. A jnani like Amma remains in *sahaja samadhi* even while performing actions; that is to say, she remains ever centered in her Self while being able to use all her human faculties easily at the same time. It is only through supreme knowledge that we can act in this way.

A story comes to mind. Once, all the animals in a forest went to see a *rishi* (seer) and asked him, "What is the difference between us and human beings?"

The rishi said, "Human beings are endowed with the faculty of discernment, using which they can elevate themselves to the level of God."

The fox asked, "What if they don't use that faculty?"

"Then you're all greater than them!"

Indeed, what elevates us from the level of animals is discernment. Acting with discernment makes us worthy of grace. To develop this faculty and attain God, our ancestors chanted and prayed upon waking, while bathing, before eating… until they went to sleep.

The reason for chanting the Brahmarpanam mantra before meals is to turn even what is considered a sensory indulgence—the act of eating—into a yajna and to see the food as *prasad*, a gift from God.

In the 15th chapter of the *Bhagavad Gita*, Lord Krishna says:

> *aham vaishvanaro bhutva praninam deham ashritah*
> *pranapana-samayukta pacamyannam catur-vidham*
>
> I am of the form of the fire of digestion in all beings, which combines with the incoming and outgoing breaths to digest and assimilate the four kinds of food.[1] (15.14)

This yajna takes place within us. Here, the Brahman of food is offered to the Brahman of digestive fire. The yajna is performed to please Brahman. Eating with such awareness can help us rise to the level of divinity.

This verse is not about food but *jnana* (sacred knowledge). A jnani acts for the welfare of the world. Because her actions are performed with awareness (of the Supreme), they become a Brahma-yajna. Here, one is saturated with the experience of the Supreme. The doer, the act of doing, and the fruit of the action are all Brahman. Whereas an ordinary person performs yajnas to fulfill some desire, a spiritual seeker strives to elevate all actions into yajna to attain *moksha* (spiritual liberation). The seeker works selflessly to benefit the world and surrenders the fruit of his actions to God. This is yajna, and it purifies the doer.

A yajna ought to be a *sadhana* (spiritual practice). Sadhana does not refer only to *japa* (repeated chanting of a mantra) and meditation but doing every action with an attitude of surrender.

---

[1] The four kinds refer to foods that are chewed, liquid or semi-solid foods that we drink or swallow, foods that are sucked, and those that are licked.

An experience I had many years ago put me on the path of surrender.

When I joined the ashram, I was assigned to do *seva* (selfless service) in the Ayurveda section. Once, when there was a lot of work, another brahmacharini and I went to the kitchen late for dinner. By then, the food was finished. The kitchen volunteers scolded us for coming late. We felt sad and upset, but felt that there was no point in explaining why we were late. Instead, we prayed: "Amma, we are very hungry! What to do now?"

Within five minutes, Amma came to the kitchen and asked who had not eaten dinner. She then asked the kitchen volunteers to make some *kanji* (rice gruel). Amma herself lit the fire, kept water to boil, and added grains to the water while chanting a mantra. She then reminded us to drink the kanji water. Once the kanji was cooked, Amma served us and then left the kitchen. Not only did our hunger get appeased, we also had an unforgettable experience!

Amma's every breath is at the service of the world. We cannot even begin to fathom in how many ways she is serving the world. Amma helps us to see that this whole universe is a *yajnashala*—an arena for performing yajna. The sun and moon give light selflessly. A tree gives shade, even while it is being felled. The cow gives milk. All of nature is imbued with the spirit of giving.

In the *Bhagavad Gita*, Lord Krishna goes so far as to say, *"Yajno danam tapashcaiva pavanani manishinam"*—"Indeed, sacrifice, charity and austerities are sanctifying even for the wise" (18.5).

In the *Ramayana*, Lord Rama tells Lakshmana, "We should perform duties that come to us, surrendering their fruits to the Supreme." Amma says the same thing in simple words:

"Everything is God alone. With this understanding, perform work with an attitude of surrender to God."

The attitude behind the action is important. This is why Arjuna's *yuddha* (war) turned into a yajna whereas Daksha's yajna turned into a yuddha. The former acted with an attitude of surrender, but the latter acted with pride and arrogance.

Amma gives us opportunities to participate in yajnas. I remember one such occasion. When the nursing staff at AIMS Hospital went on a strike, I was serving at the Paripally Orphanage. Amma telephoned me and said, "Go to AIMS immediately!"

I left for AIMS at once. I was assigned to the MICU (Medical Intensive Care Unit). The situation there was pathetic. Many nurses had deserted the patients, who were critically ill.

I was assigned four patients. Although I had studied nursing, I was unfamiliar with much of the state-of-the-art equipment. I prayed fervently: "O Amma, I don't know anything. Please act through me and see to it that no one dies!"

The nurse-in-charge told me what I had to do. By Amma's grace alone, I was able to discharge my duties and also help another nurse. Even though I had health issues and could never stay in an air-conditioned room for long, I did not think about these, and instead focused on serving the patients until the nursing staff returned. Amma saw to it that the condition of all the patients improved; no one died.

One of the patients was a 16-year-old girl with jaundice. Her mother told me that her daughter had smiled for the first time after being admitted to the MICU, so assuring had the environment been for her. I realized that we had all only been instruments in Amma's divine hands.

A jnani sees only Brahman. Adi Shankaracarya declares, *"Brahma satyam jaganmithya, jivo brahmaiva naparah"* — "Brahman is the only truth. The world is unreal. There is no difference between the individual self and Brahman" (Brahma Jnana Vali Mala, 20). When we say that the world is unreal, it does not mean that it does not exist but that it keeps changing. This is often misunderstood.

Once, a farmer sent his son to study philosophy. When he returned home after his studies, the son was silent. When the father tried speaking to him, the son said, "Father, you don't exist."

When his mother heard this, she became emotional. "How dare you say that your father does not exist? He raised you!"

Hearing her outburst, the neighbors rushed to the house. The son said, "Mother also does not exist. This house does not exist. These people also do not exist. Everything is *mithya*, a mere illusion."

The father could not tolerate this anymore. He whacked his son on his head with a stick. The son started crying in pain. The father asked him, "Why are you crying? After all, it was your non-existent father that hit you with a stick that probably doesn't exist either. So how can you feel any pain?"

Clearly, the father had mastered the rudiments of his son's philosophy!

We have wrong notions about the truth because it has not become our experience yet. Amma says, "Creation and creator are not different from each other. The creator has become the creation." We can use clay to mold the form of a donkey or horse. Though the forms are different, they are, in essence, the same. Likewise, behind the diversity of the world is the one singular principle, Brahman. Man and God are not different; they are one. The same divinity is present in each one of us. Gaining this non-dual experience is the goal of human life.

Scientists say that everything is energy. The ancient rishis went a step further: they said that everything is *chaitanya* (pure consciousness). Their experience was *'sarvam brahmamayam'*—'Brahman pervades everything.'

Amma is established in that supreme consciousness. She does not see anything as different or separate from her. Many years ago, she called all the ashram residents to the water tank. She got in and asked us to get inside as well. I immediately jumped into the water. Seeing this, Amma looked pleased! She then used a hose to pour water on everyone's head. When Amma showered me with water, she said, "I am performing *abhisheka* (ceremonial bath) to the *Brahmasthana pratishtha* (idol in the Brahmasthanam temple)." For Amma, the hose, water tank and we are Brahman alone.

It is important to chant the Brahmarpanam mantra before eating food. The thoughts of the person who cooks affect the food, and the subtle aspects of the food we eat shapes the mind. Chanting the Brahmarpanam mantra before eating the food nullifies negative effects.

What we take in through our sense organs also affects the mind. This is why we should try to hear and see only what is auspicious; hence the peace prayer: *"Bhadram karnebhih shrnuyama devah…"*—"May we hear auspicious words with our ears…" By the same logic, may all that we utter and do be auspicious, and may we consciously strive to channel Amma through our words and deeds. This attitude will help us control the mind consciously.

Dr. Frank Baranowski, a psychologist from America, has done extensive research on auras, the energy patterns that surround living beings. Once, he decided to check if chanting the

Brahmarpanam mantra had any impact on the food to be eaten. Using a Kirlian camera, he took a photo of the food before and after the mantra was chanted. The photo taken after showed a blue aura around the plate. When he asked a spiritually evolved person about this, he was told that the blue aura was an indication of how much the food had been purified.

In the *Taittiriya Upanishad*, it is said, *"Annam brahmeti vyajanat... annam na nindyat"*—"Food is Brahman... it should not be insulted." Amma says that wasting food is sheer injustice to society, as so many people are suffering from a lack of food.

Once, after chanting the Brahmarpanam mantra, Amma asked the ashram residents, "Children, what do you think of while chanting this mantra?"

One brahmacharini said, "We think of Amma."

Amma said, "It's not enough to think of Amma alone. We should also think about those in the world who do not have food. We must pray that their hunger is also appeased."

An incident that took place years later helped me reflect on what Amma said. After a public program in Mumbai, I noticed poor children from the locality fighting over the leftover food in the waste bin. This scene made me sad and helped me appreciate Amma's words anew. If we listen to and contemplate on the Guru's words, our ignorance will be dispelled, and supreme knowledge will shine forth. Just as the wind can scatter clouds obscuring the sun, the wind of divine grace can remove the clouds of mental impurities to reveal the knowledge shining brightly within.

I saw Amma for the first time in 1995. At that time, I was working in a hospital in Attapadi. A doctor there gave me the *Lalita Sahasranama* (1,000 names of the Divine Mother) book and told me about Amma. This is how I started doing *archana*, chanting the divine names. Later, I saw a photo of Amma in a shop and bought it. A Christian friend told me, "Amma is a powerful Goddess. She does not differentiate between people of different religions. If you're going to see Amma, please take me along also."

We went to Amritapuri. When I entered the Kali Temple, the pillars in the hall reminded me of the description of Manidvipa (the abode of the Goddess) in the *Devi Bhagavatam*. I saw Amma, the Goddess, in the center of the temple, surrounded by devotees singing bhajans. When I was about to reach Amma, she glanced at me. I felt as if I had known Amma for a long time. During darshan, Amma called me *"mutte"* ("pearl"). I experienced a peace I had never known before. While leaving the ashram, I had only one thought: to see Amma again and again.

I soon read Amma's biography, *Matruvani*, and other ashram publications. After reading them, the desire to stay in the ashram arose in my mind. The thought that I might not be able to stay there would sadden me.

Soon after this, by Amma's grace, I received an opportunity to work in a hospital run by a devotee of Amma. My main duty was to visit nearby villages to conduct archana and bhajans. Doing so, I used to feel strongly that I was Amma's daughter, and the villagers would also behave as if Amma was their very own. This is not surprising. In the *Lalita Sahasranama*, the Goddess is glorified as *'vishva-mata'*—'Mother of the Universe' (934).

Once, when I went to one of the villages, I conducted an archana in the local temple. Before doing the archana, I placed in front of me a photo of Amma in Devi Bhava that Amma had blessed and an issue of *Matruvani* next to the photo. After the archana, a woman approached me. Pointing excitedly at Amma's photo on the front cover of *Matruvani*, she asked who it was. When I told her it was Amma, she narrated her experience.

Two years before, some missionaries had come to convert the villagers to their religion, and had succeeded to some extent. This woman, who was the wife of the village headman, was saddened by this and told her husband that it was because there was no temple in the village that their people were such easy targets. She felt that building a temple in the village would help. That night, she dreamt of a woman dressed in white, who told her, "Daughter, don't feel sad." She then pointed to a high spot in the village and showed her an idol. It was revealed that four people, including her husband, would bring this idol down from the top of the mountain. The woman further said that these four people should observe a religious vow for 41 days before bringing the idol down. She also indicated where the idol should be installed. The headman's wife told me that the woman in white had been none other than the person on the cover of *Matruvani*!

The next day, when the headman's wife went to the spot Amma had indicated, she saw an idol of Simhavahini Devi, the Goddess seated on a lion, that no one had seen before. She was overjoyed! The whole village observed the vow for 41 days, after which they built a temple and installed the idol. Thereafter, all conversions stopped in the village. It was at this temple that I conducted the archana. When I told the headman's wife that the woman gracing the front cover of *Matruvani* was Amma, she shed tears of joy, realizing that Amma had fulfilled her sincere desire to protect Sanatana Dharma.

As for me, my sole desire was to stay in Amma's ashram. The question was, did I have what it takes to become an ashram resident? With her grace, nothing is impossible. I went to Amma's

Kodungallur Brahmasthanam program and asked her, "Please enable me to stay in your ashram."

Amma said, "Daughter, come with Amma!"

Accepting her words literally, I went and stood near Amma's car, thinking that she would take me to Amritapuri in her car! Darshan was about to end. When Amma reached the car, I told her, "Amma, I've come!" Smiling sweetly, she told me that I must inform my family members before joining the ashram. When I went home and informed my father, he said that he already knew about it. Father had a Guru, whose photo was on the altar along with two photos of Amma. The night before, father had a dream in which he saw Amma in Devi Bhava and his Guru. Amma told his Guru, "Amma will look after this family. I will take his daughter, too." That was how my father learnt that I would join the ashram. Since then, Amma has been looking after all my family members, who now regard her as their sole refuge. Later, my sister also joined the ashram.

I used to fall sick constantly. It is said, *"Purva janmakrtam paapam vyadhirupena badhate"*—"The bad actions of past births come in the form of disease." Amma has healed each of my diseases in different ways.

Once during Amma's birthday, I became giddy and started vomiting. The doctor I saw said that the problem was an imbalance in the right ear and advised me to go to AIMS Hospital. I decided to inform Amma before going. When I went for darshan, Amma told me, "Daughter, introduce these reporters here to the students from the Paripally Orphanage and tell them about the student activities in Paripally."

I agreed. When I told Amma about my dizziness and vomiting, she told me to sit next to her. A little later, when I learnt that the reporters were waiting for me, I got up. Somehow, I felt energized. I spoke at length to the reporters. After that, I ate some food and did not feel the need to go to the hospital.

The next day, when I went to see Amma, she whispered something about Paripally in my right ear. Her breath went into my ears and it felt soothing. Ever since then, I have never had any ear problem.

On another occasion, the doctor advised surgery in the nose. When I told Amma about it, she asked me which nostril, and then said, "Go to Paripally now. During the vacation, you can go to AIMS." When I went to AIMS, the doctor compared the X-ray taken earlier and the one just taken, and exclaimed in surprise, "Amma's grace! Your nasal problem has been completely healed!"

Amma has become my sole medicine and doctor. The only thing is, I must follow her prescription precisely and faithfully.

Like Amma's ever-flowing grace, experiences from her are unceasing. The Divine Mother is showering infinite love on her creation. One wonders if anyone has ever expressed unconditional love on such a scale. Amma has nothing to gain for herself, and yet, she engages in selfless action for our sake. May Amma's example inspire us all to love and serve others selflessly.

# 6

# Divine Mercy
*Br. Neelakanthamrita Chaitanya*

The Vaishnavaite[2] literature of Tamil Nadu describes the life of saints and devotees in rich detail. These biographies appeal to the masses, enabling them to assimilate lofty spiritual truths embodied by these great souls. The life of Thirukachi Nambi, an ardent devotee of Lord Vishnu and Guru of Sri Ramanujacarya,[3] is a beautiful example. Thirukachi Nambi was engaged in worshipping Lord Vishnu daily in the Varadaraja Perumal Temple in Kanchipuram, near Chennai. His devotion to Lord Vishnu was such that every night, the Lord would converse directly with him.

One day, while Nambi was fanning him, the Lord saw Shani Bhagavan[4] standing behind Nambi. Lord Vishnu realized that Saturn would soon rule Nambi's life for the next seven-and-a-half years, and that it would be a challenging time for him. Lord Vishnu warned Shani Bhagavan not to touch his dear devotee. Deferring to the Lord's wish, Shani Bhagavan requested that he be allowed to exert his influence on Nambi for seven-and-a-half months. Lord Vishnu said that even that was too long. Shani

---

[2] Literature pertaining to Lord Vishnu and his avatars.
[3] A key figure in the Vaishnavaite tradition and chief proponent of Vishishtadvaita, the philosophy of qualified non-dualism.
[4] A personification of the planet Saturn, which delivers the results of our past karma in the form of positive or negative events in our life.

Bhagavan reduced the time period to seven-and-a-half days, but the Lord did not agree to that either. Finally, Lord Vishnu allowed Shani Bhagavan to seize Nambi for seven-and-a-half hours.

In that short period, Nambi was accused of a theft he did not commit, and he was imprisoned. Later, the king realized that Nambi was innocent, released him, and begged him for forgiveness. By Lord Vishnu's intervention, Nambi's long seven-and-a-half years of karmic suffering was reduced to a brief seven-and-a-half hours.

This story illustrates the following verse in the *Bhagavad Gita*, where Lord Krishna says:

> *kshipram bhavati dharmatma shashvacchantim nigacchati*
> *kaunteya pratijanihi na me bhaktah pranashyati*
>
> Soon he becomes a noble soul and certainly attains lasting peace. O Arjuna, declare boldly that no devotee of mine is ever lost. (9.31)

In the previous verse, Lord Krishna says that even if the vilest sinners worship the Lord with exclusive devotion, they are to be considered righteous if they have repented. Amma has many devotees, who used to lead unrighteous lives, but underwent a transformation after meeting Amma and receiving her unconditional love. Some have even become residents of Amritapuri, dedicating their life to serving others and doing spiritual practices. They are living examples of Krishna's promise of redemption.

In his book *Ultimate Success*, Swami Ramakrishnananda narrates an incident that happened many years ago. There was an ardent Krishna devotee named Bhaskar, who lived about seven kilometers away from Amritapuri. One day, Bhaskar offered *payasam* (sweet pudding) to Lord Krishna's image in his house. Amma, who was giving Krishna Bhava darshan, got up and walked the entire distance to Bhaskar's house. There, she asked him for the payasam which he had just offered Krishna. The devotee was dumbfounded and realized that Amma was Lord Krishna himself.

Later, Amma permitted Bhaskar's adopted son to run a teashop inside the ashram for devotees. The young man earned a good income. After a few years, when Amma requested him to move his shop to another spot in the ashram because of space constraints, he became upset and left the ashram.

After the 2004 tsunami, he turned up at one of the ashram's relief camps. Amma noticed him and saw how malnourished he looked. She forgave him for his earlier arrogance and had a house constructed for his family. Such is her boundless compassion.

In the *Gita*, Lord Krishna tells us what kind of offering is dearest to him:

> *patram puspam phalam toyam yo me bhaktya prayacchati*
> *tadaham bhaktyupahrtam ashnami prayatatmanah*
>
> I accept even the simplest offering of a leaf, flower, fruit or water, if it is offered with devotion and a pure mind. (9.26)

Amma says that the best offering to God is the '*hrdaya-pushpam*'—'the flower of our heart.' The heart flower denotes pure love and innocence. We have heard that an innocent heart is the dwelling place of God. There are many instances from the lives of Amma's devotees that show this.

## A Recounting of Precious Moments with Amma

There was a devotee in Madurai, whose grandson was born with a congenital heart defect. Since the family could not afford the corrective surgery, Amma told them that she would arrange for the surgery to be done free at the AIMS (Amrita Institute of Medical Sciences) Hospital. As the boy was then too young to undergo a heart surgery, it was decided that it would be done after he turned three.

In the meantime, the boy grew close to Amma, and began to consider her his dearest playmate. Just before the operation, the family came to meet Amma, who lovingly assured them that the operation would go well. The little boy insisted that Amma be with him during the operation, and she affectionately agreed.

When it was time for the surgery, the boy refused to enter the operating theater until Amma came. The parents did not know what to do. Finally, a nurse told the boy, "Son, Amma is waiting for you inside the operating theater!" She thus succeeded in convincing the boy.

After the surgery, the nurses and the doctor remarked on the special fragrance that had lingered in the operating theater during the operation instead of the usual chemical smell. When the boy regained consciousness, his first question to his parents was, "Where did Amma go? She was here with me until a moment ago."

The next time they met Amma, they told her what the boy had said. Amma smiled and said, "How could I not come? He was calling out to me so intensely; I could not stay away from him!"

There was once a householder devotee who went to meet his Guru at his ashram. He prayed sincerely to the Guru to free him from the bondage of *samsara* (cycle of birth and death). The Guru was moved, and said that he would call the devotee to the ashram when the time was ripe.

A few years later, the Guru called the devotee and asked him to come and live with him at the ashram. The devotee said that as his children were still young, he would come after their marriage. Years passed. After the marriage of the children, the Guru called him again. This time, the devotee said, "I need more time. I want to spend time with my grandchildren."

Years passed and the devotee died. Because of his attachment to his family, he was reborn as a dog in the house. One day, the Guru visited the devotee's house. Recognizing the dog as his old disciple, the Guru approached him and asked him to follow him. The dog said that he needed to protect the family, which had many enemies. Eventually the dog died, and was reborn as a snake in the same house.

Out of deep compassion for his devotee, the Guru made a firm decision to save him at least in this birth. He went to the house and told the family members that there was a snake in their cupboard. He asked them to bring it to him without killing it. They did as advised, but also thrashed it. Seeing the bruised snake, the Guru told him, "You should have come to me right at the beginning, when I called you the first time!"

This story makes me wonder about Tumban and Bhakti, the ashram dogs, on whom Amma lavishes much love and attention. This does not mean we have to be born as a dog or snake to enjoy her love. What the story shows is that the Guru will never forsake us. She hears all our prayers and fulfills the pure desires of every innocent heart.

When we pray to God to fulfill our desires, we should exercise discernment, as wrong desires always bring sorrow. Once, a daughter-in-law prayed intensely to Lord Shiva for relief from her oppressive mother-in-law. Pleased with her penance, Lord Shiva appeared before her and granted her a boon. The daughter-in-law said, "Lord, please grant me three wishes."

Shiva smiled and replied, "I shall, on one condition. Whatever you ask for, your mother-in-law will get 10 times more."

The daughter-in-law agreed. For the first wish, the daughter-in-law asked for 100 *crore* (1 billion) rupees. Lord Shiva smiled and said, "So be it, but your mother-in-law will get 10 billion crores."

For her second wish, the daughter-in-law said, "I want to become Miss India."

"Alright," replied the Lord, "But your mother-in-law will become Miss Universe."

The daughter-in-law had a hard time digesting this. She thought carefully before asking for her last wish. Finally, she smiled and said, "Lord, I want a mild heart attack."

We should not pray like this. Praying to harm others makes us unfit for divine grace, as God is compassionate and loves all beings.

The following incident exemplifies Amma's all-encompassing love. Once, an old man came to meet Amma for the first time during her Chennai program. He was undergoing tremendous mental suffering and tearfully shared his sad story with Amma. After being diagnosed with stage-one leprosy, he had been treated and his disease had been cured. He even obtained a medical certificate testifying that he was completely healed but his friends and relatives shunned him and treated him as an outcast.

Amma lovingly consoled him, gave him darshan, and made him sit next to her for some time. She called Swami Vinayamritananda, who is in charge of the Chennai ashram, and asked him to give one of the houses from the free-housing project to this old man. Hearing this, the man shed tears of gratitude. "My own family members rejected me," he said. "But Amma, who did not even know me until today, accepted me and blessed me with a house!"

Even though this man was not a devotee and was meeting Amma for the very first time, she was ready to help him without any hesitation. Such is the greatness of Amma's compassion.

There is nothing that we can offer the Guru in return. She turns the business creed, 'Minimum investment, maximum returns,' on its head. Her approach reflects 'maximum investment, minimum returns.' The Guru spends all her time and effort in uplifting her devotees and disciples.

Being *purna* (complete), Amma needs nothing from anyone. She is the ocean of *sat-cit-ananda* (truth-consciousness-bliss). The scriptures say that Sage Shuka became absorbed in pure consciousness after taking just a sip of that ocean. Sage Narada, who also sipped a little of sat-cit-ananda, soared into a state of divine ecstasy. How can a mere mortal express her glory? May Amma ever dwell in our hearts.

# 7

## The Power of Words
*Br. Srikrishnamrita Chaitanya*

Amma says, "We need to develop awareness in each and every word we speak. The presiding deity of speech is fire. Speech is meant to give light and warmth to those around us. May all your words become filled with light."

What does Amma mean when she says that our words should give "light and warmth" to others? She means that our words should help the listener. They must provide hope to the demoralized, confidence to the dejected, comfort to the downtrodden, and knowledge to an inquisitive mind.

Are our words like this? Amma says that they are often like wet firewood; when kindled, it only produces dark smoke. In other words, our words hurt others.

When do words illumine? When they are motivated by compassion, harmony, kindness, affection and other positive impulses. If our thoughts are saturated with lust, anger, greed, delusion, pride and jealousy, the words emanating from such thoughts will be dark.

Words spoken carelessly can cause sorrow to others and ourselves. Therefore, every word must be uttered with utmost care. A good word can turn a foe into a friend. Likewise, the wrong word can make a close friend our biggest enemy. When somebody criticizes us, we must try not to react instinctively in anger. Instead, we ought to sit silently for a while. When the mind is still, we will be able to see our shortcomings more clearly. It is much easier to correct ourselves when we can see and accept our mistakes. Amma says there should be a gap between thought and action. The light of *viveka* (discernment) shines through that gap.

Words have the power to spur us into doing good and bad. Words can even take and give life. Amma tells the story of a beggar who begged for days but received nothing. He was starving. Unable to bear the pangs of hunger, he decided to end his life. Before taking his life, he thought, "I will beg one last time, but if I do not get anything, I will commit suicide."

He begged the next passer-by he saw. The passer-by put his hand into his pocket and exclaimed, "Oh no! I forgot to take my wallet when I left home. I'm so sorry that I have nothing to give you. But I'll come again this way. I will certainly give you something then."

The beggar replied, "Don't worry. You have already helped me. Your words gave me much comfort. I was about to commit suicide but I've decided not to. If there are people with hearts like yours, people like me have reasons to continue living."

When Amma gives darshan, she gives us happiness through all the five sense organs. The beauty of her form pleases our eyes. Her words ("Darling son/daughter") are music to the ears. Her fragrance delights the nose. The candy she gives us as prasad is sweet to the tongue. Last but not least, her warm motherly embrace gladdens both body and mind.

To focus specifically on Amma's words, we will see that when she intones maternal words of affection in our ears, we feel an indescribable inner awakening; it is as if we are reminded of the eternal and unbreakable bond with the Divine Mother. We must listen carefully to those words and meditate upon them. Those words should resound in each and every cell of our body. Amma insists on saying those few words in the mother tongue of her children, i.e. the language with which they are most familiar.

Amma's words also have the power to heal. The mantra that she gives her children is a powerful spiritual tool to help us evolve spiritually. By initiating us into a mantra, Amma says that she is imparting a part of her infinite spiritual energy to us.

Wounds on the body can heal, but wounds in the heart, i.e. those inflicted by words and thus not visible, do not heal so easily. I learnt this through an experience that I had shortly after joining the ashram. Amma assigned me the seva of teaching at the ashram's computer institute. As a young man, I had much enthusiasm. I was also immature and hot-headed. Once, I was entrusted with the responsibility of invigilating examinations, which were conducted over 10 – 12 days. During those few days, I scolded seven or eight teachers on exam duty. When Amma found out about this, she told me, "Apologize to all those you scolded!" My main seva the next day was apologizing to them. After that, Amma called me to check if I had apologized.

Amma says, "There is an aura around us that records whatever we do and say. If our words hurt others, our aura will become darker. We will suffer as a result." Through this incident, Amma taught me to be careful about how I speak to others. She also taught me to put my pride aside and bow down before others. After that, whenever I became angry with anyone, I would recall this incident and apologize to that person. Since then, Amma has not summoned me for this reason.

According to neuroscience, a single word has the power to influence the expression of genes that regulate physical and emotional stress. Positive words such as 'peace' and 'love' can alter the expression of genes, strengthen areas in the frontal lobe, and enhance the brain's cognitive functioning. They can also trigger the production of oxytocin, the neurochemical that helps induce feelings such as well-being, affinity and security.

A single negative word can increase activity in the amygdala (the brain's fear center). This increased activity releases dozens of stress-producing hormones and neurotransmitters that, in turn, impair cognitive functioning especially in the areas of logic, reason and language.

According to Sanatana Dharma, the three integral steps of scriptural study are *shravana* (listening), *manana* (reflection) and *nididhyasana* (meditation or assimilation). The first two steps depend on words.

The Upanishads explain how words ought to be. The peace invocation of the *Aitareya Upanishad* begins as follows:

> *om vang me manasi pratishthita*
> *mano me vaci pratishthitam...*

> Om, may my words be in harmony with my mind.
> May my mind be in harmony in my words...

In the *Taittiriya Upanishad*, the Guru tells a disciple who has ended his studies and is about to embark on the life of a householder, "*Satyam vada. Dharmam cara. Svadhyayanma pramadah*"—"Speak the truth. Practice dharma. Do not neglect the study of the Vedas."

The *Manusmriti* declares:

> *satyam bruyat priyam bruyat na bruyat satyam apriyam*
> *priyam ca nanritam bruyat esha dharmah sanatanah*

> Say what is true but speak in a way that it is pleasing to others. Never say a truth that is disagreeable to others. Never utter a lie even if it is pleasant. This is the eternal law. (4.138)

Let me conclude by sharing my experience in giving satsangs. I gave my first satsang about 20 years ago. In that discourse, I shared my experiences with Amma, and the talk was received well by everyone. Delighted by this response, I decided to raise the standards for my next talk. I went to the library and noted a few Sanskrit verses and their interpretations. On the morning of my talk, I sat next to Amma while she was giving darshan. When a certain man came to Amma, she told him, "Hey Hari, we don't need your Vedanta here!" Then, turning to her right, she asked me, "Isn't your name also Hari?"

"Yes," I said. Amma asked me the question so casually that I did not give much importance to it.

That night after bhajans, I delivered my talk, reading out from the papers before me. The talk was full of abstruse spiritual ideas. I imagined that it had been excellent and felt proud. Shortly afterwards, a brahmachari informed me that Swami Amritageetananda, who was the ashram's *shastra acarya* (teacher of scriptures) and satsang coordinator then, wanted to see me. I thought he wanted to commend me on my fine talk. When I went to see him, he gave me a severe scolding. It was only then that I realized that my talk had been dry and dismal. This unexpected blow shattered my pride.

Amma says that if we tell a cow that is chewing the plants in our garden, "O darling cow, please don't eat the plants," it is not going to listen to us. But if we brandish a stick and shout at it, "Go!" it will leave. Sometimes, words have to be used in this way, too.

That was also when I realized the import of Amma's words that morning. She had given me a hint that she knew all about my talk even without my saying anything to her. What need is there to tell the all-knowing Mother anything?

After this incident, I completely lost the desire to give satsangs. I do not even think about it in my wildest dreams!

May Amma give us the strength to recognize the power of words and to use them consciously and carefully.

# 8

# True Service
*Bri. Anamayamrita Chaitanya*

I first met Amma in Chennai in 1987. Later, I visited Amritapuri Ashram with my father. When we went for darshan, my father told Amma, "Please bless my daughter. She has no mother."

The expression on Amma's face became sad, and she asked with concern, "You have no mother?"

I spontaneously replied, "No, Amma. I have only you."

Amma laughed with delight. Looking around at others, she asked, "Did you hear what this daughter said?" Everyone except my father understood the exchange. When I returned to Chennai, I prayed fervently to Amma during each and every second of the next three months to let me join the ashram. I had never considered myself spiritual before, but now, I knew from the depths of my soul that I wanted only Amma. I could not explain it to myself even. I prayed, "Amma, if you allow me to join the ashram, then please tell me. I'm too scared to ask you."

I came from a typical Indian joint family, one that was warm, close-knit and loving. I was afraid that my family members might not allow me to join the ashram. I did not want any unnecessary drama around my joining the ashram, and prayed to Amma for that as well.

I returned to Amritapuri during the Vishu holidays with my whole joint family. I waited until everyone else in my family had gone for darshan before going. After hugging me, Amma looked into my eyes and asked me, "Daughter, do you want to join the ashram?"

I was stunned but nodded frantically. Amma said, "Ashram life is very difficult. Will you be able to handle it?" Again, I said a heartfelt yes. Then Amma said, "Okay then, join the ashram."

The whole exchange did not take long, and no one in my family noticed what had transpired. My family members left the next day; I told them I would return in two days. Later, I informed them over the phone that I had joined the ashram and would not be returning home.

I went on tours with Amma, attended bhajans, and immersed myself in other spiritual practices. Just before Amma left for her World Tour, the swami in charge of the Chennai ashram told Amma that I had not completed my postgraduate degree. He suggested that I complete it as it would be useful to the ashram. Amma told me to complete it and return.

On my way back to Chennai, I was feeling nervous. Ever since I informed my family members about my joining the ashram, I had not contacted any one of them. Back then, there were no mobile phones or the Internet. I never imagined that I would have to return home. But now, after just two months, I was returning to complete my degree. I feared that when they saw me, they would hit the roof. I could not imagine them agreeing to help me complete my degree or allowing me to return to the ashram. But when I reached home, there was no outburst or scolding. Though my family looked astonished to see me, they welcomed me warmly. When I told them that Amma had asked me to finish my studies, they immediately made the necessary arrangements. Later, my grandmother told me that during his morning prayers, my eldest uncle had a vision of Amma, who told him, "My daughter is returning today to finish her studies. You should help her. No one should scold her." When he told my grandparents about his vision, they dismissed it as a figment of his imagination. When I showed up in person, they were stunned. Their faith in Amma also grew. From then on, they supported my joining the ashram. Only my father, not realizing how serious I was about ashram life, was against my decision. So, when the time came to leave Chennai, I had to do so without his knowledge or permission. Later, by Amma's grace, he, too, came around and gave me his blessings.

Thus, Amma removed all the obstacles standing in the way of my joining the ashram. Later, as I continued my life on the path of renunciation, my understanding of *karma yoga* gave me more maturity. On this subject, Lord Krishna says,

> *buddhiyukto jahatiha ubhe sukrta dushkrte*
> *tasmad yogaya yujyasva yogah karmasu kaushalam*
>
> Endowed with the wisdom of even-mindedness, one abandons both good and evil deeds. Therefore, dedicate yourself to yoga. Yoga is skill in action. (*Bhagavad Gita*, 2.50)

Two verses before, the Lord had introduced the concept of yoga to Arjuna: *samatvam yoga ucyate*—yoga is even-mindedness. Here, he introduces another aspect of yoga: *yogah karmasu kaushalam*—yoga is skill in action.

What exactly is karma? What is karma yoga? Karma is action. Any mental or physical activity is karma. Karma is what keeps the world going. In the *Bhagavad Gita*, the Lord says, "No one can exist even for an instant without performing action, for all are helplessly driven to activity by their very nature" (3.5).

Karma yoga essentially means to act without the sense of being the doer, dedicating the action to God, and not desiring the fruit of the action. By dedicating what we do to God, we renounce the ego. The karma yogi feels he is able to act by the Lord's power alone. Therefore, he does not feel proud when he is praised, nor does he get upset when criticized. Such an action becomes sanctified and does not bind.

The *jnani* (knower of the Truth) acts but is still within. Look at Amma; she is ever engaged in work but never loses her poise. Even after long hours of giving satsangs, singing bhajans, giving darshan, and guiding managers in her organizations, she remains fresh and ready to continue serving. Clearly, Amma does not feel the burden of her duties. She does everything with great love and enthusiasm.

When Lord Krishna tells Arjuna to cast off the fruits of good and bad deeds (*"jahatiha ubhe sukrta dushkrte"*), he is encouraging Arjuna to rise above both *punya* (merit) and *paapa* (sin), which are the *adrishta phala* (unseen fruits) of every action. By doing karma for its own sake instead of acting with the desire for a particular outcome, we can bypass punya and paapa, and thus transcend the karmic cycle.

Karma yoga fosters *citta-shuddhi* (mental purity). Amma says, "For the body to be healthy, it should move and exert itself. But for a healthy mind, it should be still." However, our minds are never still. Through constant mental activity, we lose our peace of mind and happiness. This restlessness is the nature of the mind and is born of ignorance and impurity. Karma yoga helps to purify the mind.

Once we start engaging in karma yoga, we will begin to see the huge accumulation of dirt within — our *vasanas* (latent tendencies) and weaknesses. Amma says that when we sweep a room, only a small amount of dirt or dust might be seen; the room might even look clean. But when we mop the room, all the unseen dirt becomes visible.

Once, when a brahmacharini asked if it was better to focus on spiritual practices instead of seva, Amma said, "Daughter, never ever lose any opportunity to do seva. To practice spiritual disciplines, you need a still mind. One can never attain a still mind without inner purity."

Amma then told her the story of two competing artists. Each one was given a wall to display his artwork. The first artist painted a breath-taking mural of a waterfall. The second rubbed and polished the opposite wall over and over again until it began to shine like a mirror. The mural on the opposite wall was reflected on this wall but it had a special beauty as it reflected light as well. The judges awarded the prize to the second artist. Amma said to the brahmacharini, "The entire power of creation is reflected in a still mind. To attain this stillness, you must engage in karma yoga."

Many spiritual aspirants feel that work is a distraction from spiritual practices. However, if we look at Amma, we will see that she never misses an opportunity to serve the world. Whether an earthquake, tsunami, flood, hurricane or a pandemic, Amma always rushes to help. Her skillful and efficient plans for disaster management have been acknowledged even by the UN as the road map for disaster response. Yet, Amma does not have any sense of doer-ship.

She tells a story of a saint who performed many good deeds. Pleased with him, God offered him entry into heaven, untold riches on earth, and other such boons, but the saint declined them all. When he was pressed into asking for something, the saint replied, "If you really want me to accept a boon, then grant that I should always serve others and do good but in such a way that I'm not aware of it."

God granted him the boon. From then onwards, wherever the man's shadow fell, good things happened. However, the saint remained unaware of the power of his shadow to bestow happiness. People started calling him 'Shadow Saint.' We, too, ought to strive to become like this humble samaritan.

When Amma assigns us any seva, we must give up the sense of being a doer and embrace instead the idea of being her instrument. Sometimes, this means being Krishna's flute, which produces soul-stirring melodies. But there are times when we must become Kali's sword, especially if we are in leadership positions and have to make hard decisions, say, as parents or managers. To me, being Kali's sword is more terrifying than coming under it. On such occasions, humility and remembering that we are mere instruments in God's hands will help us gain courage and strength.

In a chessboard, each piece plays a particular role and can move only in a certain way. The bishop moves only diagonally, the castle, in straight lines, and the knight, one step to the side and two to the front. What if the knight thinks, "Why is the player moving me two steps back and one to the left? I want to go forward." A skillful player moves with the aim of winning. So, a step back could well be a winning move.

## A Recounting of Precious Moments with Amma

During my seva at AIMS Hospital, I have often perceived Amma's will manifesting itself. Gradually, I came to understand that she is always listening to and protecting me. There was no burden I could hide from her. I also understood that Amma is helping us do our work with strength and compassion, two components of dharma. A karma yogi must be mentally strong and compassionate.

I recall an incident that occurred shortly after the 2004 tsunami. Amma summoned me to her room. When I arrived, she was looking grim. She said, "I received a complaint about you." That morning, we had distributed new and donated clothes to the villagers staying in our camps. When we had finished giving everything away, a woman who was in the camp but who had not joined the line was brought to us by one of her neighbors. The neighbor requested us to give this woman some clothes. We did not have anything except a few torn items. We apologized and promised to bring her new clothes the next day. But the complaint that went to Amma was that we had insulted the village women. When I tried explaining to Amma what had actually happened, she cut me short sternly: "Please don't argue. You should have asked them to wait, and gone to the other camps to get her some clothes. You shouldn't have bluntly said there was nothing."

I realized that I had done wrong and apologized. Amma's tone softened, "Daughter, you're all strangers to the villagers. They've been here for decades. You should try to understand their ways first. Do you know who that woman is?"

My heart started thudding, as I tried to think of who it was I had offended. Was she Amma's relative? A childhood friend? Or one of the women who had been kind to Amma during her sadhana period?

Amma said, "That daughter and her family have been against the ashram from the very beginning. They created many problems for the ashram when it was first founded. They even filed a legal case against us in the High Court."

When I heard this, I became angry with the woman. What a terrible person she was!

Amma's next words took my breath away. She said, "Suppose you've been against the ashram all your life and had maligned it at every chance you got. Now suddenly, because of the tsunami, which took everything away from you, you have to go to a camp, where you have to stand in a line to ask representatives of the ashram, 'May I have a sari? Can you please give me a towel?' Imagine how much your heart will be hurting and how sad you will be feeling. That is why that woman didn't join the line. But she didn't have anything other than the clothes she was wearing. How could you turn her away, daughter?"

Amma's eyes filled with tears. Seeing this, my eyes, too, welled up with tears. I became speechless when I realized how deep Amma's love and compassion were.

She continued, "Daughter, normally when one person gives something to another, we consider the giver higher than the receiver. But as spiritual aspirants, we should always remember that those who give us an opportunity to serve them are helping us greatly. It is not enough to serve people. We must serve with love, compassion and sensitivity."

Amma's words shook me to the core. Since then, I have been trying to live by them.

One of the mantras in the *Lalita Sahasranama* (1,000 names of the Divine Mother) is *'Om kushalayai namah'*—'Salutations to the Divine Mother, who is skillful' (436). What is skill? It is proficiency in any action developed as a result of attentiveness or long practice. But mere technical skill is not what is meant. A karma yogi develops both the external skill as well as the correct attitude. As the yogi's mind becomes purer, his faculty of discernment becomes sharper.

Amma is not just skillful in bringing out our talents, she also deftly guides our minds without our knowing in order to bring about an inner spiritual transformation. In his book, *Color of the Rainbow*, Swami Amritaswarupananda says that managing a company of 500 people effectively means managing 500 minds. To do that well, we must first learn to manage our own mind efficiently. Let me share an experience that illustrates Amma's superb management skills.

Once, shortly after Amma landed in Europe, she called me at 2 a.m. I was delighted to receive a call from her but surprised, too, as the reason for the call did not seem pressing. Still, I listened attentively. After speaking for some time, Amma became silent but did not hang up. I, too, waited. A minute later, Amma asked about my health. After answering her, I asked her about her health and the tour. Even after that, Amma did not hang up. The thought crossed my mind, "Maybe Amma is waiting for me to ask her something." I said, "Amma, there are two graduation ceremonies the day after tomorrow and the day after that. We need your blessings…"

Before I could say another word, Amma said, "Darling daughter… kisses…" and ended the call. I scolded myself for telling Amma unnecessary things. But I had mentioned those functions only because I was feeling a little anxious about them, even though we conduct them every year. I had prayed to Amma for her grace before I went to bed that night.

The next day, I became busy with preparations for the functions. As the hospital's industrial workshop, which usually helps with stage decorations, had indicated that it would not be able to help this time, we outsourced the stage decoration to professional decorators. The decor was to be entirely floral. Apart from a flowerbed in front of the stage, the walls of the stage were to be adorned with long strings of marigold. However, the decorators who were supposed to come by 4 p.m. arrived only at 10 p.m. One of them explained that the flowers, which were coming from Tamil Nadu, had not arrived yet as the border had been closed owing to some problems. He had brought some flowers from a local vendor. When I checked, I saw that the flowerbed was fine, but the strung-up flowers were rotting. There was no way we could use them, but the stage would look stark with just a curtain. I told him to set up just the flowerbed. He did so and left. I knew that the organizers would never accept a bare backdrop. It was already midnight. The program would start at 9 a.m. and the invited guests would arrive by 7:30 a.m. There was no one to help other than two girls from my office. My heart started to beat fast. I did not know how to solve the problem. I took a deep breath and told myself, "Amma knows about the programs. I told her last night. She won't let anything go wrong." I prayed fervently for strength and ideas.

Suddenly, I remembered how Amma had used empty rice sacks as curtains for makeshift showers and toilets erected during *Amritavarsham50*, Amma's 50th birthday celebrations. Was there something I could re-purpose as stage decorations?

I took two helpers to the store. We saw some old garden ornaments. We cut off the terracotta bells and made several long garlands out of them. It was 4 a.m. How to put up the decorations on the 15-foot stage walls without workers?

I recalled how, during one of Amma's North Indian tours, she had made the brahmacharinis climb on top of the buses to do the loading. That memory boosted my confidence. We quickly set up the tallest ladder and proceeded with decorating the stage. Though I was unfamiliar with the work, by Amma's grace, we were able to finish by daybreak. The final cleaning of the stage got over as the organizers arrived. Seeing the unique stage decor, they complimented us.

We made our own decorations the next day also and put them up ourselves. On both days, the programs unfolded smoothly. Every time I felt overwhelmed, I thought of Amma's phone call. My heart filled with gratitude as I finally realized why Amma had called me — to instill in me the confidence that she was with me and would provide guidance on how to deal with any problem.

May Amma inspire us all to serve the world selflessly. May our actions help us gain mental purity. May we ultimately attain the supreme goal of life.

# 9

# Best Friend
*Bri. Prabhavamrita Chaitanya*

In the *Bhagavad Gita*, Lord Krishna explains that the nature of the world is eternal sorrow. He teaches how one can face life boldly and achieve success. His teachings help us delve deeply into spirituality and enable us to fulfill our duties in life with calm and composure. He also warns against forming attachments:

> *dhyayato vishayanpumsah sangasteshupajayate*
> *sangatsanjayate kamah kamatkrodho'bhijayate*

> When the mind dwells on an object, it develops an attachment to it. From attachment arises desire, and from desire arises anger... (2.62)

> *krodhad-bhavati sammohah sammohat smrti-vibhramah*
> *smrti-bhramshad buddhi-nasho buddhi-nashat pranashyati*

> ...from anger arises delusion, which leads to a loss of memory; a loss of memory leads to an impairment of the intellect, which leads to one's ruin. (2.63)

One of the classic examples of this degradation is found in the *Ramayana*. Kaikeyi was a virtuous queen, fond of Lord Rama. However, her mind was corrupted by Manthara, her maid, who convinced her that her own son, Bharata, should be crowned instead of Rama, and insinuated that Kaikeyi's standing would be diminished if Rama became king. By contemplating this idea, Kaikeyi became attached to it. When Dasharatha tried to thwart her plan, she became enraged and demanded that Rama be exiled to the forest, and refused to budge even when she knew that Dasharatha would die if separated from Rama.

Such incidents are not a thing of the past; they continue to take place even today. The poison of anger can kill even the purest relationship in the world—that between mother and child. Such tragedies occur because people live without any control over their sense organs. One who relishes the things of the world will not find inner bliss so easily, whereas one who restrains the mind and senses judiciously will be able to progress spiritually. One's real enemy is the extroverted mind; conversely, an introverted mind, one that is established in one's own true nature, is one's best friend.

Lord Krishna says as much:

*bandhur atmatmanas tasya yenatmaivatmana jitah*
*anatmanas tu shatrutve vartetatmaiva shatruvat*

The mind is the friend of one who has tamed it and the worst enemy of one who has not. (6.6)

We might feel that we have made significant progress in restraining our mind and senses, but we must never underestimate the insidiousness of the ego and let our guard down. Our likes and dislikes can arise at any time. Amma says they will remain with us until the last step on the road to Self-realization. No one but a liberated soul is out of danger.

Amma tells the story of a frog to explain how dangerous it is to allow the mind to wallow in sensory pleasures. A frog fell into a pot of water on the stove. The frog was basking in the warmth of the water. But as it became hotter, it became unbearable. It tried hard to get out of the pot but failed and died as a result.

Spiritual seekers must always steer clear of circumstances that threaten their spiritual growth. As Amma says, one who is addicted to alcohol will not be able to quit the habit if he keeps a bottle of alcohol under his pillow.

Frustrated desire leads to anger. Sometimes, we might approach the Guru with our ideas and plans. If she opposes them, we might be disappointed; we might even get angry with the Guru and begin to see her in a negative light. This will lead only to our downfall.

Amma says that maintaining a daily regimen of spiritual practices is of utmost importance and that it is like a shield that will protect us from falling prey to unwanted desires. She gives the example of how a tender sapling needs to be fenced to protect it from predators. Once it grows into a tree, the fencing is no longer needed and even elephants can be tethered to the tree trunk. Amma also compares the world and its attractions to an array of mouth-watering dishes. We can resist them only with the spiritual strength gained from regular spiritual practices.

What removes the taste for sense enjoyment completely is knowledge of our true self. The Self, which is of the nature of *sat-cit-ananda* (existence-consciousness-bliss), is beyond the reach of worldly attractions. Once we are firmly rooted in the Self, the mind will remain unwavering. Contemplating the Guru's words and adhering to her instructions take us to the Self. Discernment is vital.

We might try hard to exercise our discretion but still fail because our thoughts are not under our control. Just as Arjuna

## A Recounting of Precious Moments with Amma

surrendered his lot to Lord Krishna, who became his charioteer and guided him, we should let Amma control the reins of the horses of our sense organs, i.e. let our intellect be guided by her, so that she can take us to the goal of Self-realization.

Before meeting Amma, I did not know anything about spirituality, *sannyasa* (monasticism) or the Guru. The only contact I had with religion was temple visits and TV serials on the *Ramayana* and *Mahabharata*. I had also heard a few Puranic stories from elders.

Once, a neighbor told me about Amma. She was all gaga! She said that Amma was Parashakti, the supreme power. I wondered if she was a bit crazy because I could not understand how a human being could be God.

Then, one day, a copy of the *Bhagavad Gita* appeared on my shelf. It was the first time I saw that book. To this day, I don't know how it came to be there. When I read it, I realized that there was much more to life than what I had dreamt. Until then, I had only aspired to gain a good education, find a job, and lead a family life. In the meantime, my father brought home a copy of *Matruvani*, the ashram's monthly magazine. In it, I saw an article on the *Gita*. I felt that I could learn more about the *Gita* if I associated myself with Amma and her ashram. With my father's permission, I went to Amritapuri with my neighbor and her family for darshan in 2001.

Before that, I had heard some rumors about Amma although I never took them seriously. One of them was that Amma traps people with sacred ash! As I neared her, I became a little nervous and started praying to God to keep me away if Amma was not genuine. She gave me darshan. As I got up to leave after darshan, Amma pulled me back for another hug!

We then went to the bookstall. I bought a couple of books, including the *Lalita Sahasranama* (1,000 names of the Divine Mother), which I thought I would chant daily as a spiritual practice. From the *Lalita Sahasranama* book, I learned about *manasa puja*, worship through visualization. Until then, I had seen puja being done only in temples. We attended the evening bhajans, which I enjoyed immensely.

When I returned home, I started reading the books. I realized that there was much more to Amma than I had previously imagined. I had not been able to perceive her divinity because of my preconceived notions. An elderly person asked me if I could see Amma as my Guru. I said I could. That was good enough, he said. Still, I did not know who a Guru was or anything about the greatness of a Guru. My simple understanding was that a Guru was a teacher of spiritual matters.

I started doing manasa puja the very next day. I closed my eyes and tried to visualize Devi in my mind, but could not. I went to the nearest temple and bought a beautiful picture of Devi. That day, I did manasa puja to that image of Devi. As I could not see Amma as a Goddess, I imagined her to be my Guru and chanted Amma's *dhyana shloka* (benedictory verse).

I read that Amma had said that if we cannot see her as a Goddess, we can visualize any deity we like. I did not recite Amma's *Ashtottaram* (108 attributes) then, only the *Lalita Sahasranama*.

When I went to see Amma for the second time, I wondered why it was that I alone could not see her as a Goddess. Nothing spectacular happened during that darshan either.

Later, I went through a difficult patch. No one could help me. I thought, "Amma has removed the sorrows of so many people.

Can't she remove mine also?" I took out Amma's photo and started praying and crying to her.

I went to Amritapuri once again with the help of my neighbor. I was eager to see Amma and tell her all my problems. When I came before her, Amma put my head on her shoulder and caressed me. She kept telling me not to worry. My mind became peaceful. She asked me to sit by her side. After some time, I realized that I had not told her about my problems. How could she solve them if I did not tell her about them? The next day, during Devi Bhava darshan, Amma gave me a mantra.

While returning home, I felt that I had failed in my mission and that I was going back to those problems. As soon as I reached home, a girl who knew all about my problems came running to me and said that all of them had been resolved. On inquiry, I learned that the changes had taken place at around 11:30 – 11:45 a.m., the time I had Amma's darshan! All my problems had been wiped away in a moment, that, too, without my telling Amma about them! Praying in temples had brought about results, but never as fast as this. I felt that Amma, the Goddess, was far more powerful than the ones in temples!

Thereafter, I encountered a series of such experiences and realized that Amma's hands were guiding me.

There was one more reason for my choosing this path. Since childhood, I had a habit of getting stressed, sometimes for no reason! I used to imagine things and get tense. I tried different ways to kick this habit but nothing worked. Finally, Amma showed me how to keep tensions at bay. A thinking mind is like a turbulent sea, but in its depth, the sea is silent and peaceful. I realized that through constant practice and Amma's grace, we can attain that state of deep inner tranquility. This also drew me to Amma.

Since joining the ashram, I have been trying to practice Amma's spiritual instructions. She repeatedly stresses the importance of developing an attitude of acceptance. In my early days here, some of the brahmacharinis used to be sent to various Amrita Vidyalayams (schools). Some of us would also be sent to schools outside Kerala for the CBSE (Central Board of Secondary Education) inspections. When I heard that my name had been suggested for this task, I was not willing to accept it readily. Nevertheless, I did not say no. I wanted to do Amma's will. I felt that she would be pleased if I accepted assignments without reservation. Whenever I faced situations that I could not welcome readily, I would pray to Amma to show me its positive side and she would respond promptly! Whenever I accepted situations and proceeded with the understanding that Amma was taking care of me and my actions every moment, I would feel happy and content. I find that this is the only way to make life smooth.

I want to become a tool in Amma's hands. I do not have any special ability at all. During my college days, I used to worry about this, but after reaching Amma's abode, I began to see my lack of talent as a blessing. They say that God can help the blind see and the lame scale mountains. With that in mind, I have become more relaxed. I take one step to Amma, and she takes a thousand steps towards me!

Amma says that those who have surrendered totally to God will not have to seek anything. Everything they need will reach them. I used to recall these words, especially when I was away from Amritapuri and needed the support and help of many people. I felt Amma's grace though these people, but reminded myself not to get attached to them as they cannot lead me to the goal of eternal peace. Moreover, Amma says that a friend today may become an enemy tomorrow. We must have gratitude, love and respect for such people, but depend solely on Amma. If we need something else tomorrow, we can trust that Amma will send someone else to fulfill that need.

Swami Amritaswarupananda says, "In Amma's presence, what we need is an open mind. Grace will flow to us if we are receptive."

Let us cultivate the habit of watching our mind always and telling Amma everything. May Amma become our best friend and soul mate. We can pray to her to help us remove even the slightest mental restlessness. We do not even need language to talk to her. Swami Purnamritananda says that Amma has imparted much knowledge to him through silence, the language of love and the heart. Distance does not hinder communication either.

In the bhajan *'Kanniral Kanna,'* the poet sings:

> *kavalay eppozhum jnan irunitumpol*
> *durasthanallennu tonnum*
> *kannan bahysthanallennu tonnum*

> Whenever I have been vigilant, I have felt that the Lord is neither far away nor outside me.

Amma says, "The true wonder is not Krishna's lifting of the Govardhana Hill but how he uplifted the *gopis* (milkmaids) through love." She is doing the same thing, transforming the mind of each one of us. This is Amma's most wondrous act.

How blessed we are to live in the shade of her love! What can we give Amma in return for the love and compassion she is showering on us? Nothing, but we can try to surrender ourselves to the Divine. O Amma, may all our thoughts, words and deeds express your sweet will. Please make us your flute so that we can dissolve in your sweet music. Please make us humble instruments in your mission of reinstating *dharma* (righteousness), peace and happiness in the world.

# 10

## Unfulfilled Desire Leads to Anger
### Bri. Amritatmika Chaitanya

The *Bhagavad Gita* maps the career of anger — its birth and trajectory:

> *dhyayato vishayanpumsah sangasteshu-pajayate*
> *sangat sanjayate kamah kamat krodho'bhijayate*
> *krodhad bhavati sammohah sammohat smrti-vibhramah*
> *smrti-bhramshad buddhi-nasho, buddhi-nashat pranashyati*

> Pondering on sense objects, man develops attachment to them. From attachment springs the desire to possess the objects, and desire gives rise to anger.
> From anger arises delusion, and from delusion, a bewilderment of memory. When the memory is bewildered, discriminative intelligence is destroyed. This loss of intelligence leads man to complete ruin. (2.62 – 63)

A couple were celebrating their 25th wedding anniversary. The husband noticed three handsome, hand-knitted wool hats and $8,000 on the table. His curiosity aroused, he asked his wife about the items on the table.

She said, "Whenever you became angry with me and made me sad, I knitted a hat."

The husband felt very proud thinking that in 25 years of marriage, he had become angry with and hurt his wife only three times.

"Alright," he said, "but what about the $8,000?"

The wife smiled and replied, "That's the money earned from all the hats I sold!"

Like the man in the story, we are unaware of how we much hurt others when we are angry. This harmful emotion, which enslaves many of us, adversely affects us physically and mentally. When we get angry, our body produces stress hormones such as adrenaline and cortisol. Anger is one of the main causes for depression, migraine, high blood pressure, ulcer and heart disease. It also weakens the immune system.

Why do we get angry? According to the *Gita*, desire is the cause of anger. Every day, newspapers report crimes committed in fits of anger. I read a news-story about a software engineer who killed her mother and stabbed her brother because they opposed her relationship with a man. In the light of the *Gita*, we can see that the young woman developed an attachment to a man, whom she had not known before, by constantly thinking about him. From this attachment arose the desire to make him hers. When the mother and brother opposed this desire, she became angry with them. Her anger clouded her judgment, causing her to see her mother and brother as enemies. She was no longer able to tell right from wrong. When her intellect became impaired, the woman killed her mother and stabbed her brother.

The ancient Indian epics also highlight the dangers of anger. In the *Ramayana*, we see how Queen Kaikeyi, who loved Lord Rama as her own son, eventually banished him to the forest. How did this happen? Manthara, her maid, insinuated that if Rama became king, she would lose her place in the kingdom and that only if Bharata were crowned would her position in the kingdom be safe. Ruminating over the idea, she became persuaded and asked King Dasharatha for the boons he had promised her earlier. When Dasharatha did not agree to her demands, Kaikeyi became angry and lost her sense of discernment. Her anger eventually led to Rama's exile. Anger can drive away our inner divinity and thus destroy our life.

Unchecked desire turns into greed, which is the cause of many problems in society. A businessman, who was the founder chairman of one of India's biggest IT companies, once said in an interview that his ambition was to have offices in 50 countries employing more than 50,000 people. He was later charged with several offences, including criminal conspiracy, breach of trust, and forgery, and sentenced to imprisonment for several years. His company was acquired by another company, and he lost everything.

Tulsidas, the 16th-century saint and composer of *Ramacharitmanas*, a poetic biography of Lord Rama, described anger, greed, fear and worry as mental diseases. We are generally aware of physical ailments and usually take medicines to heal ourselves. But do we even recognize our mental maladies? It is important to become aware of them and then take steps to remedy them so that we can enjoy happiness and good mental health.

The *Sri Guru Granth Sahib* says, '*Mera Baid Guru Govinda*'—'My Guru is my healer.' In his book *On the Road to Freedom*, Swami Paramatmananda writes that just as there are three types of doctors, there are three types of Gurus. The first doctor advises the patient and sends him away. The second type of doctor diagnoses the illness and prescribes medicine. The third and best type not only diagnoses the illness; he even forces the medicine down the patient's throat, knowing that the patient might not take it otherwise. Amma belongs to the third category of Gurus. In her infinite compassion, Amma forcefully treats our ailments.

This reminds me of an incident. One of the students at Amrita Vishwa Vidyapeetham (Amrita University) was addicted to smoking. He even skipped classes to smoke. If anyone advised him against it, he would get angry. This habit led him to bad company. Eventually, he was suspended from the university for a breach of discipline. He became distraught and did not know what to do.

Someone told him to go to Amma and shed crocodile tears; she would revoke the suspension. He went to Amma, prepared to act, but when he reached her, he started crying naturally. Amma spoke to him like a friend. The student was touched by her approach. Slowly, he established a bond with Amma and began to share all his secrets with her.

When he saw that all Amma wanted was his own good, he started heeding her advice. He worked hard to quit smoking and was finally able to give it up. When he could not find a job, he turned to Amma, who gave him a job at the university. Then she advised him to pursue a degree in Management. He joined Amrita University's Business School and was eventually placed in a good company. Since that first encounter, he continues to seek guidance from Amma in all areas of his life.

Amma says that anger is like a sharp knife without a handle; it injures both the person who is wielding it and the one who is attacked. But if we can heal ourselves of anger, it can bring about a change in others, too. An incident from my life illustrates this.

The first *seva* Amma assigned me was teaching at Amrita University. Later, from 2015, Amma asked me to travel around

## A Recounting of Precious Moments with Amma

the country to conduct AYUDH and IAM™ (Integrated Amrita Meditation) programs.

While at the university, I was also the Vice-Chairperson of a department. Once, when I recommended that a student who had not registered for the examinations be allowed to register even though the registration deadline was over, my superior, who was a stickler for rules, became displeased. The issue was brought to Amma, who spoke to my supervisor and resolved the issue. But he remained angry with me. I also became angry with him for opposing me. A few days later, when Amma brought up the issue again, I told her that I was not speaking to him any more as he was angry with me. She said, "Speak to him and resolve the standoff."

My anger towards him dissipated quickly. The next day, there was a festive celebration at the university on the occasion of Onam. I went up to my superior and spoke to him casually, as if nothing had happened. He was taken aback. For some time, he did not say anything. Finally, he said, "The best thing about this Onam is that you spoke to me. It makes me very happy!"

This incident helped me appreciate Amma's advice that if we use our discernment, keep an open mind, and interact with others patiently, we can bring about changes both in ourselves and in others.

We must learn to discriminate between reaction and response. If we observe our mind, we will come to understand that we often regard people and situations with preconceived notions. When people do not act according to our wish, we get angry. We expect everyone to speak to and behave with us lovingly. When that expectation is not met, we react with anger.

However, we also know how to refrain from reacting in certain situations. Amma cites the example of how, when reprimanded by our boss, most of us will not react, even if we are angry, because we know that we might lose our job, if we do so. So, we rein in our anger and respond calmly. This seeming calmness is only a suppression of anger. We might express it later at home, towards our spouse or children.

The Greek philosopher Aristotle once said, "Anybody can become angry—that is easy; but to be angry with the right person, and to the right degree, and at the right time, and for the right purpose, and in the right way—that is not within everyone's power and is not easy."

When asked about anger management, Thomas Paine, an 18th-century author, revolutionary and philosopher, famously said, "The greatest remedy for anger is delay."

Both pieces of advice reveal three qualities that Amma asks us to cultivate: awareness, witnessing and listening. If we can practice the witness attitude, we can acquire a mind that reflects the feelings and emotions of others.

The most powerful medicine that Amma prescribes for gaining the witness attitude, for controlling anger, and for responding properly (and not reacting) is meditation. In all the meditation techniques that Amma teaches, be it the IAM™ or Ma-Om meditation, we are asked to focus our attention on our breath. There is a close connection between our breath and the mind. When we are angry, we breathe rapidly, and when we are happy and relaxed, our breathing is more even and slow. Amma teaches us that we can calm the mind by regulating our breathing carefully.

Medical science has shown that when we are happy, the brain's left prefrontal cortex is relatively more active. Conversely, when we are sad, depressed or angry, the right prefrontal cortex is more active. Meditation increases activity in the left prefrontal cortex and reduces activity on the right side.

Once during a program, a woman spoke to me about the benefits of IAM™: "It has brought so much peace in my life!" I was happy to hear it and asked her how long she had been practicing the IAM™. She said, "I don't practice it, but my husband does. He was an extremely short-tempered person before learning the meditation. Practicing the IAM™ technique has reduced his anger so much that my life has become peaceful now!"

An experience I had while teaching meditation taught me how dangerous a clouded mind is. Once, on the eve of an IAM™ training course for people from various business firms, I learnt that trainers from another organization that teaches meditation worldwide wanted to attend the program. My fear was that they wanted to copy Amma's techniques and make it theirs. As Amma was on her US tour, I emailed Swamiji (Swami Amritaswarupananda) for guidance. He asked me to find out why they wanted to attend the IAM™ course when they had their own path and meditation. I asked but did not receive a proper reply. Swamiji said that it was not proper to prevent them from participating and that I should not say no.

I then prayed to Amma to stop them from coming by ensuring that they get stuck in a traffic jam! She answered half my prayer. They did get stuck in traffic and arrived late, after the relaxation exercises had ended. I told one of the organizers to tell them that as they were late and had not signed the non-disclosure form, they would not receive the practice handouts.

After the training, they congratulated me, gave me a memento, and spoke very lovingly. I spoke to them in a smooth and polished manner, but my heart was closed to them.

When Amma returned from the tour, I went to give her the memento. Amma was surprised when she learnt that they had come for the IAM™ training. "It's surprising. They don't usually go to other organizations." When I told Amma that I had not given them the handouts, she was displeased. Amma said that I had done wrong and should have given them the handouts. I felt bad when I realized that because of my ego and preconceived judgments, I had acted contrary to what Amma would have wanted. Amma has equal love for all. That is how she is able to bring about a transformation in millions of people throughout the world.

The sense objects ('*vishaya*') mentioned in the verse quoted at the beginning can also be a circumstance or environment that pampers our ego. The egocentric mind likes to be indulged. If we are not careful, our attachment to such circumstances can lead to anger when our desires are thwarted. The Guru will give us hints and warnings. If we pick up on them, we will be able to correct ourselves before it is too late. Over the years, I have learnt that Amma's warnings can take many forms: a pointed glance, change of expression, silence, a comment, a knowing smile... When Amma speaks, the *sankalpa* (divine resolve) behind her words brings about an understanding.

Many years ago, another brahmacharini and I attended a week-long technical training at IIT (Indian Institute of Technology), Mumbai. As we had to leave immediately after Amma's birthday celebration, we could not see her before she left for her Europe Tour. I was feeling sad about it. When we reached Mumbai, news came that Amma had watched a Sanskrit play in which I was to have played a character called 'Madhyaman.' Someone told Amma that Madhyaman had left for Mumbai. I had missed all that fun and joy of being with Amma, and this thought made me even sadder. My longing to see Amma increased.

To my great surprise, on the last day of our training, a devotee in Mumbai called to say that Amma was transiting in Mumbai on her way to Europe. She reached the airport in the evening, but as we did not have a pass to enter the airport, we waited outside. We prayed intensely to be able to meet Amma just once before she left. Finally, late at night, Amma came out. Seeing us waiting there, Amma gave us darshan and spoke to us briefly. She mentioned that she had watched the Sanskrit play.

Just before Amma got into the car that would take her from the domestic to the international terminal, she turned to me and asked, "What's your *vishayam* here?"

In Malayalam, the word 'vishayam' ordinarily means 'topic.' I answered "Computer programming." Amma smiled.

It seemed like a casual question, but when Amma's car pulled out, I felt as if a lightning bolt had struck my mind. I sensed that she had meant something else when she used the word vishayam. During the training, the conference delegates had received 'five-star' treatment. The training was being conducted on Amrita's A-View platform, a product developed by Amrita University. As we were from Amrita, we found ourselves in situations that boosted our ego.

When I contemplated on this, I understood that all thoughts and circumstances that boost our ego, which we think about constantly and develop attachment to, are vishaya. Unknowingly, we develop a craving to enjoy the same circumstances again.

For many days, Amma's words continued to resound in my mind. Contemplating on them has helped me to gain more awareness and a witness attitude to a certain extent, especially when I am in similar situations.

Modern medicine offers many remedies for afflictions of the mind. The ancient scriptures also prescribe remedies for these problems. But the most practical and permanent solution that can help us transcend the afflictions of anger, desire and greed is surrendering to the master.

Someone asked a *mahatma* (spiritually illumined soul), "What is the difference between following a Guru and following the scriptures?"

He replied, "It's simply the difference between sugarcane juice and the leftover dry pulp. There will be some sweetness in the dry pulp, but the essence is in the juice. The essence of all the scriptures and knowledge is in the Guru. So, those who wish to get rid of the diseases of the mind and want to be happy and peaceful must surrender to the Guru."

At the end of each chapter of the *Bhagavad Gita*, we chant,

> *sarva dharman parityajya mamekam sharanam vraja*
>
> Relinquish all your material duties and surrender completely to Me alone. (18.66)

This verse shows that despite following instructions and striving hard, we understand that our efforts are limited. By Amma's grace, may we all be able to surrender ourselves to her and thus rid ourselves of our mental ailments.

# 11

## Lighting the Lamp of Love and Wisdom
*Bri. Medhamrita Chaitanya*

Once, a reporter asked Amma a few questions. She answered all of them with a minimum of words. The reporter was astonished and asked, "Amma, my questions were very long. How could you answer them so succinctly?"

Amma said, "A small key is enough to open a big box."

Similarly, in Amma's Ma-Om Meditation technique, through the simple but mindful repetition of the sacred syllables Ma and Om, we can unlock our inner treasure—pure existence, knowledge and bliss—which is our real nature. In this way, Amma is helping us find the answer to the age-old question, "Who am I?" Meditation is the method to unravel this mystery.

Amma often says, "Meditation is as precious as gold." When the mind becomes still, subtle and introverted through meditation, we will be able to attain the most precious gem: Self-realization. Amma's Ma-Om Meditation technique helps to calm the mind. Ramana Maharshi says, "When we inquire into who we are, all other thoughts subside, and the Self is revealed."

Once, there was a big party. The party-goers were talking, laughing, eating and drinking. Meanwhile, a stranger turned up and he seemed busier than everyone else. The others began to notice him and, suspecting that he was a gatecrasher, started asking around about his identity. Realizing that people were watching him, the stranger left the place quietly.

This is also the case with our mind. If we do not pay attention to our thoughts, they will dominate us. But if we start observing them, they will subside and disappear.

The ascetics of yore attained spiritual liberation through practices such as the *pancagni tapasya*[5] or by standing on one leg for eons. We do not have to do such arduous *sadhana* (spiritual practices). Amma is taking us towards the same goal through the simple Ma-Om Meditation technique.

It is an easy way to calm the mind. There is no need to sit in the *padmasana* (lotus posture) or any other yogic pose. The meditation can be practiced sitting in a chair.

Some may wonder if it is possible to reach the ultimate goal by practicing such a simple technique. In this context, I remember a devotee asking Amma, "Why do you give so much importance to drinking *kanji* (rice gruel) water along with each meal?"

Amma replied, "If Amma's children follow even one of her instructions, then she can save them." From this, we can understand that even if Amma's advice appears insignificant, the benefits of following it are far-reaching.

The Ma-Om Meditation technique starts with observing the breath. The mind and breath are interconnected. Observing our breath slows down and regulates our breathing, and this in turn calms the mind.

---

[5] Literally, 'five-fire penance.' It is a form of meditation in which the seeker meditates with fires burning on all four sides; the fifth fire is the sun above. The seeker must tolerate the heat in order to gain one-pointed concentration.

Amma also says that Ma represents divine love and Om represents divine light. Love and light form the substratum of the universe.

What would the world be like if there were no love? The conflicts in homes and between countries arise from a lack of love. Murder and suicide also take place for the same reason.

Similarly, what would the world be like without light? Suppose the sun, which gives us energy, did not rise. Flowers will not blossom. We will not survive for long. In countries where the sun shines for only a few hours a day, the incidence of depression is greater compared with other countries. If sunlight plays such a vital role in physical life, then the light of knowledge plays an even more significant role in the spiritual life.

In the Ma-Om Meditation technique, Ma represents the path of devotion and Om represents the path of knowledge. Once, Amma asked, "Are devotion and knowledge one or are they different?"

A brahmacharini replied, "They are different." When Amma wanted her to elaborate, she said, "In devotion, there is duality: God and the devotee are separate. But in knowledge, only the Self exists."

Amma said that one can attain knowledge only through devotion, and that ultimately, both are one and the same. Both paths lead to the same goal. Only if we have love within can we see all as one; only if we have this vision can we love the entire creation. Therefore, love and light are always together. They can be compared to inhaling and exhaling—both are vital phases in breathing.

The devotion of great *bhaktas* (devotees) like Radha, Andal and Meerabai started with pure love for Lord Krishna, and culminated in the knowledge that the Lord dwells in everything and everyone, including themselves.

Once, a devotee asked Amma, "Are love and meditation different?"

Amma said, "Those who think that love and meditation are different haven't understood the depth and meaning of either. When love deepens, it naturally becomes meditation. Love is the power that helps the flower of meditation blossom and spread its fragrance everywhere."

In pure love, there is no expectation. One loves for love's sake. The following incident from the life of Swami Vivekananda illustrates this. His Guru, Sri Ramakrishna Paramahamsa, used to wait daily to see his dear disciple. One day, when Narendra (Swami Vivekananda's pre-monastic name) came, he found Sri Ramakrishna sitting in the hall and talking to his other disciples. He did not even turn to look at Narendra, who remained seated until evening and then left. The same thing happened again when he returned the next day. Two weeks passed in this way. Though there was no change in Sri Ramakrishna's behavior, Narendra continued to visit him and listen to his master's satsangs attentively. Seeing this, the Guru's heart melted with compassion. He came to Narendra and affectionately asked him, "For the last two weeks, I did not talk to you or even look at you. Yet, you continue coming here. Why?"

Narendra's reply was beautiful. "I don't care if you talk to me or not. I come here only because I love you."

Hearing the disciple's reply, Ramakrishna Paramahamsa was overjoyed.

A similar incident took place in the lives of two senior swamis in Amma's ashram. In the olden days, some householder devotees felt that Amma was showing too much love to them and asked her not to do so. Amma agreed. From that day onwards, whenever Br. Balu (now Swami Amritaswarupananda) and Br. Sree (now Swami Purnamritananda) came to see Amma, she would not even look at them. Seeing this, the householder devotees were pleased. They thought, "Amma heeded our words!"

Days passed. Br. Balu and Br. Sree continued to visit Amma every day. Seeing her indifference to them, they were deeply saddened. They would prostrate to Amma and then go into the *kalari* to meditate. One day, they were so overwhelmed by grief that they silently shed tears while meditating on Amma. Unbeknownst to them, Amma was watching them. She went to them, hugged the two of them and cried with them.

Amma then explained the reason for her earlier behavior. "Even if Amma doesn't speak to you, she knows that you will continue to come and see her. Amma enacted this drama to show the devotees the greatness of the love you have for her."

The Guru's love, compassion and wisdom are continuously flowing toward creation. To receive them, we must become worthy. The story of Appoothiyadigal, a devotee of Lord Shiva, is illustrative. Appoothiyadigal was very devoted to his Guru, Thirunavukkarasar, though he had never met him. He built many shelters for Shiva pilgrims and provided food and water to them in the name of his Guru. He even named his children First Thirunavukkarasar, Second Thirunavukkarasar…

Once, when Thirunavukkarasar visited Appoothiyadigal's village, he noticed his name written on many shelters. Upon inquiring, he learned that a devotee was behind this. Thirunavukkarasar decided to visit Appoothiyadigal's house in the guise of a Shiva devotee.

Whenever Appoothiyadigal saw a Shiva devotee, he would greet him with respect and love. Wanting to test his devotion, the Guru started speaking contemptuously about Thirunavukkarasar. Although Appoothiyadigal felt hurt and sad, he kept quiet as his aim was to serve Shiva devotees. He sent his elder son to pluck a plantain leaf. When the son went out on this errand, a snake bit him and he died. Appoothiyadigal felt that if he revealed what had happened, the guest would not partake of food from his house. So, both husband and wife covered the dead body of their son with a leaf and decided not to tell their guest about it. When he was invited to have lunch, the guest insisted that the couple's children join him. He specifically asked for their eldest son. Appoothiyadigal said that he was not available. But when the guest insisted that he be summoned, Appoothiyadigal had no choice but to explain what had happened.

Thirunavukkarasar called out the son's name. To the surprise of Appoothiyadigal and his wife, the dead son sat up, as if he had just woken up from sleep. That was when Appoothiyadigal and his wife realized that their guest was none other than their venerable Guru, Thirunavukkarasar, himself.

A reporter once asked Amma, "Amma, don't you feel bored giving darshan like this every day?"

Amma replied, "Where there is love, there can never be boredom."

One of my friends who is a musician told me that whenever she sits for meditation, she finds it difficult to concentrate because of back pain. But when she sits for bhajans, she completely forgets the discomfort in her back. Sometimes an entire hour will go by without her realizing it. Why? It is because of her love for music. When we love something, it becomes effortless.

## A Recounting of Precious Moments with Amma

Just as my friend loves music but not meditation, most people have likes and dislikes. But Amma has equal love for everyone and everything—devotee and non-devotee alike; both those who worship her and those who criticize her. There are so many incidents in Amma's life that show her equal and unconditional love for everyone. She is truly an embodiment of love.

Let us now look at what Amma says about light, which denotes knowledge, wisdom and awareness.

In the *Brhadaranyaka Upanishad*, there is a conversation between Yajnavalkya, the Guru, and King Janaka, the disciple. Janaka asks, "What serves as light for man?"

"Sunlight," answers the Guru.

"When the sun has set, what serves as his light?"

"Moonlight."

"What if there is no moonlight?"

"Fire serves as his light."

"What if the fire has gone out?"

"Sound serves as his light."

"What if there is no sound?"

"The Self serves as his light," replied Yajnavalkya. "It is by the light of the Self that man sits, moves, works and rests. The Self is our knowledge and strength."

Knowledge is like a flame. Just as the brightness of the flame does not diminish even when many lamps are lit from it, sharing knowledge with others does not reduce it in any way.

What the Upanishad refers to as the 'light of the Self,' Amma calls awareness. She says, "Awareness is the torch within us." A seeker who has awareness and discernment will never stray away from the spiritual path but will be guided by the Self.

In contrast, a lack of awareness creates problems not only for us but for the people around us as well. Once, four friends were walking in a forest and came upon a skeleton. Three of them had special skills and were conceited about them. The first man could recognize which animal's skeleton it was; it was a lion's. The second man could give form to that animal. The third man could infuse life into the form. When they tried to bring the skeleton back to life, the fourth man, who did not have any special skills but who was discerning, warned his friends not to do so, but they did not heed his advice. The fourth man climbed up a tree. The other three men brought back to life the dead lion, which killed the three friends.

The first three men had knowledge, but knowledge without discernment is harmful. That is why Amma says, "We have information but no awareness."

Once, a brahmacharini from Tamil Nadu asked me to write a letter to Amma in Malayalam. By Amma's grace, I could read and write Malayalam to some extent. After the scriptural class, we sat in the balcony of the Kali Temple, just across Amma's room. My friend told me what she wanted included and I was trying to translate it. Soon, we started arguing heatedly what about what to include in the letter.

Suddenly, we heard a loud bang from Amma's room. Somehow, both of us sensed that we were doing something wrong, but as we were both new to the ashram then, we were not sure. Nevertheless, we moved away and did not disclose what had happened to anyone.

Later, someone told us that it was Amma who had slammed the door shut. When I heard this, I felt bad. The next day, I went for darshan and apologized to Amma for being noisy near her room.

Amma smiled compassionately and advised me: "You need to be aware while doing each and every action. Although you were talking about Amma, you should take into consideration the time and place when you do something. Don't waste the early morning hours in unnecessary talk. Dedicate that time to sadhana."

I am still trying to follow the precious teaching Amma gave me that day.

Even a single word from Amma can uplift one's life. This is because words from a *mahatma* (spiritually illumined soul) are like fire, kindling knowledge within.

My family first met Amma in Chennai in 1988. When my father went for darshan, Amma told him to come to the ashram with his whole family. This was a turning point in our lives. Since then, Amma has been our sole refuge. Amma has always been with us when we faced problems. Even today, she continues to guide us in all things, big and small. We need not even tell her anything. Amma protects us in the same way that eyelids protect the eyes.

She is the embodiment of Ma and Om. For decades, Amma has been traveling around the world, lighting the lamp of love and wisdom in human hearts. Innumerable lives have been transformed by her grace.

To uplift ourselves, all we need to do is enshrine Amma in the temple of our hearts. May we all be able to attain divine love and light, and thus fulfill our lives.

# 12

# Love and Light
*Br. Gurupadamrita Chaitanya*

How wonderful this world is! Behind the innumerable links and chains in creation is a glorious interplay of divine love and dynamic intelligence.

All beings—human beings, birds and beasts, plants and trees—are ever engaged in action. There is no life without activity. Any action presupposes *iccha-shakti* (willpower), *jnana-shakti* (the power of knowledge) and *kriya-shakti* (the power of action). In the *Sri Lalita Sahasranama*, the thousand names of the Divine Mother, she is acclaimed as *iccha-shakti jnana-shakti kriya-shakti svarupini*—the embodiment of the powers of will, knowledge and action. She is also called *premarupa* (the form of love) and *nityabuddha* (one with awakened intelligence). When we do any work, we ought to do it with love so as to enjoy it. To ensure that we do it well, we should also work with awareness. These two qualities—love and light (of awareness)—are vital in life.

*Mahatmas* (spiritually illumined souls) express selfless love. They also know their Self. They understand the nature of life and how to live in the world. Amma is an embodiment of *prema* (love) and *bodha-prakasha* (light of awareness). In the *Ashtottaram* (108 attributes) on Amma, she is hailed as *purna-brahma-svarupini*—the complete manifestation of the Absolute Truth. She is also called Premamritanandamayi—full of divine love and immortal bliss. The former is the first of the 108 attributes and the latter, the last. The mantras in between relate the divine play around Amma's spiritual practices and service activities. This package of 108 attributes reveals how pure awareness and love have come together to uplift the world.

Whenever Amma gives a satsang, she begins with the following words: "*Premasvarupigalum atmasvarupigalumaya ellavarkkum namaskaram*"—"Prostrations to all of you, who are the very embodiments of supreme love and the supreme self."

Amma sees everyone as an embodiment of love and the Self. Do we see this? Do we have the same purity of love, dedication, sacrifice, discernment and other such virtues Amma demonstrates? No. Why? What is preventing us from expressing those noble qualities in all their fullness? It is our ego—the sense of 'I' and 'mine.' It is as if we have lit a lamp and then kept it hidden inside a pot.

In general, worldly love is predicated on duality. Such love is also fraught with expectation. When the expectation is not met, sorrow or hatred arises. In contrast, in true love, there is no 'I' and 'you,' only love. Therefore, there is only happiness.

Amma says that in true love, the one who expresses love enjoys happiness the most. The heart of one who gives love is like a well that fills with more water as water is drawn from it; it gets filled with ever more happiness. When we give some food to a poor and hungry boy and watch him eat it with relish, how happy we will feel; and how pure that happiness will be. Having tasted that satisfaction, we will feel inspired to do more good deeds.

It is the nature of love to flow outward and not to stagnate. In *Amritadhara*, a poetic rendition of Amma's teachings, she says:

Love is not a personal property.
It is the strength of the heart.
If prevented from flowing out, it will become putrid.
If we start sharing it, it will never be exhausted.
Love will not be diminished if shared.
Love is fullness.

Amma is a deluge of love. She flows on, causing the flowers of peace, happiness, goodness and well-being to blossom everywhere. Love is natural in a person of spiritual realization. That is why Amma is a friend to all in creation. She sees everyone and everything around her as different expressions of the same self.

We can understand this better by observing Amma giving darshan. When someone who is sad comes to Amma, she reflects that person's sorrow. When someone else comes to tell her the good news that he has received a good job offer, Amma reflects the joy he feels. The reason behind this empathy is Amma's awareness of her spiritual oneness with them. From this, we can understand that *jnana* (knowledge) and *bhakti* (devotion) are not two separate entities, but two sides of the same coin.

In a bhajan that Amma sings, love is associated with the Shakti, the feminine principle of dynamism, and light is associated with Shiva, the masculine principle of quiescence:

> *cittatarcalikkave kriyatmakatvashakti ni*
> *nishcalam vasikkave shivatvamennarijnjnitam*
> *shaktiyum shivatvavum parasparanupurakam*
> *buddhiyekkavijnjna veda tattvasarame tozham*

O Shakti, you are the creative power that arises when the intellect stirs. When the mind is perfectly still, we can understand the Shiva principle. Shiva and Shakti are complementary. I bow down to you, who transcends the intellect and who is the essence of the Vedas.

In Amma's 'Ma-Om Meditation' technique, the meditator synchronizes the inhalation with the silent intoning of 'Ma,' and the exhalation with 'Om.' This technique allows one to regulate one's *prana* (vital breath) and bring the vacillations of the mind under control. 'Ma' denotes love and 'Om' denotes light. When one consciously begins to associate the breathing with feelings of love and light, the inner absorption in meditation becomes even deeper.

There is 'Ma' in 'Om.'[6] This suggests that light (of true knowledge) encompasses love, that jnana and bhakti eventually converge.

The principles of love and light are important for any seeker aiming to progress spiritually. To attain the goal, one must have both determination and a clear idea about what it takes to reach it. This dedication itself will kindle the inner light.

A Guru told his disciple to retrieve the precious gems hidden in a cave. When the disciple reached the cave, he realized that he needed a lamp to find the gems. Similarly, hidden inside the cave of our heart are the gems of peace and happiness. To find them, we need the light of awareness, which will help to awaken the love lying dormant within us.

We can see love in its lower sense in human relationships and desires. Awareness elevates and purifies it, making it holy.

---

[6] Om is actually AUM, and the mantra is made up of 'A-kara,' 'U-kara' and 'Ma-kara;' i.e. the sounds A, U and Ma.

Amma says, "Awareness is like fire; even if you hold the candle downwards, the flame will always taper upwards."

Before Tulsidas became a saint and the illustrious poet of *Ramcharitmanas*, a retelling of the Sanskrit *Ramayana* in the Awadhi language, he was excessively attached to his wife. Once, unable to curb his desire for his wife, who had gone to visit her parents, Tulsidas braved heavy rains and climbed up to her room, using a snake he mistook for a rope. Seeing this, his wife sneered, "If only you had such love for Sri Rama, you would have been spiritually liberated!" This stinging rebuke acted as an awakening. Tulsidas renounced worldly life and became an ascetic.

Many saints attained Self-realization through the path of love. Tulsidas and Surdas are two examples. The first step in the path of love is *'shravana,'* listening to the names and glories of the Lord. It is the first part in the nine-fold path of devotion known as *nava-vidha-bhakti*, which also encompasses *kirtana* (singing the glories of the Lord), *smarana* (remembering him), *pada-sevana* (serving him), *archana* (worshipping him), *vandana* (prostrating to him), *dasya* (having the attitude of a servant towards him), *sakhya* (friendship with him) and *atma-nivedana* (self-surrender).

Shravana helps to sow the seed of love for God. By listening to the names and glories of God, the devotee can feel love and light. Shravana kindles bhakti and fosters a fondness for holy company. No one has realized God without bhakti and only through jnana. Only one who has love can attain the ultimate. The *gopis* (milkmaids) of Vrindavan beheld Krishna everywhere and eventually became one with him only because of their pure love. Love attains fullness only with knowledge. Radha's love was already informed by knowledge. This is evident in every story that

Amma narrates about her. Amma is trying to uplift us from the level of gopi-bhakti to that of Radha-bhakti.

Surdas,[7] who was born blind, had intense love for Krishna. Once, he stumbled into a ditch. He began singing praises of Sri Krishna, who appeared, lifted Surdas out of the ditch, and blessed him with vision. Seeing his beloved Lord's beautiful form, Surdas became overwhelmed by bliss. He said, "O Lord, now that I have seen you, I have no desire whatsoever to see the world of delusion. Please take back my power of seeing." Surdas became blind again but remained content because he had enjoyed the vision of the Lord.

Surdas's love for Krishna was paramount and indescribable. However, in the case of most aspirants, the love and light they feel are still underdeveloped. Trying to feel a greater intensity of love and striving for total awareness are part of their *sadhana* (spiritual practice). The sincerity of our efforts makes us worthy of divine grace. This is where *karma yoga*[8] becomes relevant. We must exercise *shraddha* (attentiveness) while doing any work. Doing so will awaken awareness within us. When we work selflessly and lovingly, as if our work were a worship of the Divine, our minds will gradually become purified. In due course, love and light will blossom within us.

All those who have met Amma are blessed. Her every word, deed, touch and glance are filled with love and light. Having met her, many have become inspired to attain God realization. Such is my case.

I first met Amma in Palakkad when she came to bless the foundation stone for a Rama temple. I had gone there with one

---

[7] Sixteenth century devotional poet.
[8] Path of dedicating all action to God.

of my friends. Amma smiled at me from a distance, and I felt powerfully drawn to her. I could not wait to have her darshan.

Soon after that, I came to Amritapuri for darshan. From then on, I started visiting the ashram regularly. After landing a job in a school, I started visiting every week. I would leave Palakkad on Thursday night and reach Amritapuri on Friday morning. I would leave after Devi Bhava darshan on Sunday and go to school directly on Monday morning. This habit did not go down well with either my family members or the school authorities. Even Amma warned me, "Don't keep coming here like this..." But I disregarded her advice.

I kept asking her if I could join the ashram. However, even after five years of repeatedly seeking her permission, Amma did not yield. I felt that it was because I did not obey her. I stopped visiting Amritapuri for quite some time.

The next time I visited was on Onam. During my previous visits, I would come with all the things necessary to stay in the ashram permanently. But on that day, I had brought only one set of clothes and other necessities. While waiting in line, I decided to ask Amma again if I could stay in the ashram. I did. Amma asked, "What is it, daughter? What did you say?" I repeated my request. Amma relented.

After some time, I began to feel that I ought to have submitted a resignation letter to the school. I informed Amma about this and went to the school. My plan was to go to the school, submit the letter, and return immediately. But the school's headmaster informed my family members, who took me home forcibly and locked me in a room.

I started looking for ways to escape but failed. My next tactic was to act as if I had lost all interest in joining the ashram. I started behaving in a friendly and loving manner towards my family. They let me out of the room. I stole some money from my father's pocket.

One day, all my family members went out. I had told my mother that I would prepare curry for lunch that day. Thinking that I was busy in the kitchen, my mother became engrossed in talking to a neighbor. I silently left the house, took a bus to Palakkad city, and took another bus from there to Thrissur. There, I boarded a train and came to Amritapuri.

The next day, my father came to the ashram, looking for me, but I hid myself. He had to leave without finding me. My family life had been haunted by some long-term and unresolved problems. My mother had never been healthy enough to take care of me or show me much love. As a result, I had developed certain mental problems.

Amma has healed me of all these problems through the innumerable loving glances she gave me. I often feel that she had been trying to pour love into me, but I was like an upturned bowl that could not receive even a drop of her grace. I used to worry a lot about this. Over time, I became aware of my shortcomings and have improved from the time I joined the ashram. It was Amma's grace alone that enabled this transformation.

Amma's first and final resort in any endeavor to uplift people is love. She uses the same love that draws people to her to refine them. If we compare our mental condition when we first met Amma to what it is now, we will understand how successful true love is. She loves everyone selflessly. Everyone who comes to her gets a strong feeling that Amma is his or her true mother.

Amma runs many service activities for the uplift of society. Both her vision of life and her work are informed by love and the light of awareness. For this reason, only someone like Amma can truly uplift the world.

We are all on the path to perfection; our love for Amma is taking us there. Her grace is ever flowing towards us, but our own impurities might prevent us from receiving it. May Amma bless us all with the dedication to purify our hearts and surrender to the Supreme.

# 13

# Fragrance of Love and Knowledge
*Bri. Neeragamrita Chaitanya*

Is there anyone in the world who does not meditate? When we are hungry, we meditate on food. When we feel sleepy, we begin to lose awareness of the external world and start meditating on sleep. A robber meditates on what he wants to steal. A suckling infant meditates on its mother. A beast meditates on its prey. A crane stands in meditative stillness on the banks of the river. All of nature is ever in meditation.

As part of the Ma-Om Meditation technique, Amma instructs us to concentrate on the flow of our breath, and to synchronize the 'Ma' sound mentally with our inhalation and the 'Om' sound with our exhalation. Ma denotes the principle of love and Om denotes the light of knowledge. When we meditate intently on love and light, we become one with them.

Amma says that the Self is of the nature of love. That is why she says that the conventional expression, "I love you," ought to give way to "I am love." What is real love? Our relationship with our parents, relatives and friends is limited to the physical and emotional levels. Most of us consider this love, but it is only attachment. It is the lowest rung on the ladder of love. Instead of remaining there, we must climb higher until we attain ultimate love. In that state, pure love becomes a meditative state of oneness.

Great artists experience a little of this pure love. Some dancers and musicians forget themselves in their art, and even merge into the ecstatic state of oneness with the dance, song or music. However, this union with their art is temporary. When the dance or music stops, the meditative experience of oneness also ceases.

There have been great souls whose love was so exalted that they abided in a permanent state of oneness. There was no duality in the love between Radha and Krishna. They were spiritually one. Radha exists in Krishna and vice versa. During Amma's visit to Vrindavan, we noticed that people greeted each other as "Radhe…" They had the awareness that where Radha is, there Krishna also is. This is true love.

The body-mind complex is a wondrous phenomenon, but we know only its most superficial level. We can achieve anything through the body and mind. As part of certain religious festivals, devotees walk barefoot on live embers. They have no body consciousness while doing so, and do not experience any pain during or after the ceremony; they do not suffer from burns either.

The body is made up of the five elements (*pancabhuta*), namely earth, water, fire, air and space. But the mind can transcend these elements and thus rise above body consciousness.

Amma is a living wonder who is established in that state of transcendence. Her darshan is proof of this. Amma has received devotees for a stretch of more than 20 hours, a feat that is humanly impossible. As Amma herself has said, "If this body were made of gold or steel, it would have worn out long ago." What enables Amma to rise above body consciousness is her unconditional love for all.

Amma often says that we have information but no awareness, as a result of which, we fail to reach the goal of life. We think one thing, say something else, and act in a way that is at odds with what we think or say. We must bring awareness into our thoughts, words and deeds.

Every packet of cigarette has a statutory warning printed clearly on it: 'Smoking cigarettes is injurious to health.' Those who smoke see it and yet continue to light up. But when they are diagnosed with cancer, an awareness of the injuriousness of smoking dawns in them and helps them quit smoking. Even if they feel like smoking, they will control the urge because they now know that smoking will lead to their death. That is why Amma says, "The lack of awareness is the cause of wrong actions."

Amma narrates the story of a thief who asked a Guru to help him stop stealing: "Please bless me. I want to quit my bad habit. But stealing is my livelihood."

The Guru said, "If you cannot stop stealing, then you must inform the owner about what you intend to steal before stealing it or tell him what you stole after the act."

The thief agreed. One day, he broke into a house. He opened the cupboard and was about to steal an expensive ornament when he suddenly recalled the Guru's words. But if he informed the owner, the owner would call the police, who would jail him. The thief withdrew his hand. Even though he felt tempted to steal, the thought of the consequences stopped him.

The same thing happened day after day. Finally, the thief went to the Guru and asked him, "What kind of advice did you give me? If I inform the owner before or after the robbery, how can I get away with stealing?"

The Guru said, "You came to me because you wanted to quit stealing. That's why I gave you that advice. When you remembered my words, you became aware of the consequences of stealing and was thus able to desist." If we are aware of the consequences of our actions, we will not commit any mistake.

The easy way to bring awareness into each and every action is through meditation. Meditation is not just sitting with eyes closed but maintaining constant awareness. Each thought is like a small drop of water. A small stream can be dammed easily, but not so a river of thoughts. So, we must be watchful of our thoughts. Thoughts can manifest as words, which, in turn, can lead to action. If the mold is defective, all the items made from that mold will be faulty. Likewise, if we do not correct our thoughts, then the words and actions arising from them will create problems. Only meditation can help us control the mind.

During the initial stages of meditation, we need to practice chanting Ma and Om mentally while inhaling and exhaling. As we are breathing all the time, we can make it a practice to synchronize Ma and Om with your breath all the time, regardless of what we are doing. With sufficient practice, we will be able to intone these sounds continuously, and not just during meditation. Practicing this constantly will make it second nature to us.

The scriptures say that passing away while chanting Om will liberate us spiritually:

> *om ityekaksharam brahma vyaharan mam anusmaran*
> *yah prayati tyajan deham sa yati paramam gatim*
>
> One who quits the body while remembering me (God) and while chanting Om will attain the supreme goal. (*Bhagavad Gita*, 8.13)

Thus, through this simple meditation technique, Amma is leading all of us to liberation, the state of oneness with the totality. Love and light represent the principle of Advaita (non-duality).

After the December 2004 tsunami, many people who had lost their homes and loved ones came for darshan and poured their hearts out to Amma. When she consoled them and wiped away their tears, Amma would cry along with them. Seeing this, a reporter asked her, "Amma is considered an embodiment of Advaita. Why then does Amma cry when people express their sorrows?"

Amma immediately replied, "This is Amma's Advaita." She perceives everyone as her own self. Hence, she feels the joys and sorrows of others as her own.

Once, a Guru asked his disciples, "How do you know when the night has ended and the day has begun?"

One disciple said, "When one is able to identify the object seen through the window as a tree." The Guru shook his head in disagreement.

Another disciple said, "When one is able to differentiate between a tree and a human being."

"No," said the Guru.

Yet another disciple said, "When one can distinguish between man and woman."

Guru said, "None of your answers is correct. Night ends and day begins only when we see every woman as our own mother or sister and every man as our own father or brother."

The awareness of kinship spontaneously gives rise to an attitude of love and generosity. This is the motivation behind Amma's innumerable good works. The former President of India, Dr. A.P.J. Abdul Kalam, said during his visit to Amritapuri, "Amma's life conveys the message of giving and going on giving. She finds joy in giving. Her hand always reaches out to the needy."

Most recently, Amma contributed to both the central and state governments in their fight against the coronavirus. The Ashram also distributed thousands of masks, which Amma herself helped to stitch. Likewise, we need to think about what we can give society.

Once, a traveler saw a beautiful mansion and stood enjoying its beauty for some time. A man came out of the mansion and asked the traveler, "Why are you standing here? Are you admiring this mansion? Did you like it?"

The traveler nodded his head in affirmation. The man said, "It's mine."

The traveler said, "I'm happy to hear that."

The man said, "My elder brother built it for me."

"How nice!"

"You're probably thinking, 'If only I had an elder brother like that,' right?"

"No, I was thinking, 'If only I could be like your elder brother.'"

Like the traveler, we should always think about what we can do for others. God always gives us opportunities to serve others according to our capacities. Therefore, we ought to see Amma's humanitarian activities as golden opportunities for us to serve others. Amma does not need anything from us. That said, we must not forget our duty to society.

Amma speaks about a devotee from Kozhikode who sells lime juice to earn his living. He sets aside some money daily to buy lemons for the next day and for Amma. At the end of every month, he visits Amritapuri and offers the small sum of money he has saved to Amma. Whenever she speaks about him, her eyes well up with tears of love. I have no doubt that this devotee has earned a lot of merit and grace.

By trying to do good always and by seeing only the good in others, we can experience the light of peace within. A story illustrates this.

Once, there lived a king who had only one leg and one eye. He commissioned artists to paint a beautiful portrait of him. The artists did not dare to take on the assignment, as they did not know how they could paint a 'beautiful' picture of a one-eyed and one-legged man. Finally, one artist agreed. Everyone wondered what kind of a portrait he would paint. To everyone's surprise and to the king's immense satisfaction, he painted the king hunting in the forest with one leg bent and one eye closed, as if he were aiming his arrow at an animal! Like this artist, let us try to see only the good in others and not their weakness.

Pure love brings about an inner transformation. The transformation of a bud into a flower is imperceptible because the change happens very slowly. When the bud blossoms, the flower will be fragrant and beautiful. If we try to force the bud open, it will lose its beauty and fragrance. Only nature can bring about this unfurling in the best way. Likewise, all change should be prompted by the heart and not forced upon us by any external agency.

Once, a couple came to Amritapuri. Both the husband and wife were spiritually inclined but the husband was a devotee of Sri Ramakrishna Paramahamsa and never went to Amma for darshan. His wife, a devotee of Amma, felt sad about this and told Amma, who said, "Don't worry, daughter. He thinks we're different. It's okay."

When the wife told her husband what Amma had said, he conceded that he saw Amma and Sri Ramakrishna differently. But as days passed, there was a change in him, as he was constantly accompanying his wife to Amritapuri. The veil of ignorance became finer. After some time, he started going for Amma's darshan and this created a yearning in him. He wanted to be in her presence all the time. Amma never showed him any special attention. One day, unable to curb his devotion to Amma, he asked her, "Amma, can you give me a mantra?"

Amma smiled at him and asked, "Son, who is your favorite deity?"

Tears welled up in his eyes. He said, "Please don't ask me about my favorite deity. Sri Ramakrishna Paramahamsa is my life but I cannot live without you, Amma!"

Amma understood his pain. She said, "Son, you don't need the mantra of any deity. The spiritual principle is enough for you. I will give you a mantra accordingly."

By Amma's grace, the devotee's dualistic perceptions gradually resolved into an understanding of oneness. In a similar manner, by the Guru's grace, a disciple lacking in virtue can blossom into one redolent with the fragrance of love and knowledge. Only a Satguru like Amma can bring about this transformation. Meditating on Amma, who is the embodiment of light and love, can bring out the love and knowledge in us. May we all be able to attain the highest form of meditation.

# 14

# Ever in Amma's Service
### Bri. Samaradhyamrita Chaitanya

One day, the Lord was sitting by the banks of River Yamuna and chatting with the *gopis* (milkmaids). He suddenly asked them, "What do you do when you feel sorrowful?"

They said, "O Lord, as soon as we think of you, all our pain and sorrow fly away. When your adorable face illumines our heart, how can there be a place for sorrow?"

In the *Narada Bhakti Sutra*, Sage Narada says that the gopis had *prema-bhakti* (loving devotion) for Lord Krishna. In the book, the sage elucidates the nature of true devotion: *"sa tasmin paramaprema rupa"*—"Devotion is supreme love towards God" (2); *"anirvacaniyam premasvarupam"*—"the nature of true love cannot be described" (51).

What is the state of someone who has gained such devotion? *"Yallabdhva puman siddho bhavati amrito bhavati trpto bhavati"*—"Attaining devotion makes one a perfected soul, immortal and content" (4).

Further, Sage Narada says, *"Yajnatva matto bhavati stabdho bhavati atmaramo bhavati"*—"Experiencing it, one becomes divinely inebriated, remains perfectly still, and revels in the Self" (6).

In the *Bhagavad Gita*, Lord Krishna alludes to *gauna-bhakti* (lower devotion) and *para-bhakti* (higher devotion):

*catur-vidha bhajante mam janah sukrtino'rjuna*
*artto jijnasur artharthi jnani ca bharatarshabha*

O Arjuna, four types of pious people worship me: the distressed, seekers of knowledge, seekers of material gain, and knowers of the Truth. (7.16)

Amma demonstrates para-bhakti. During her early days of *sadhana* (spiritual practices), she would chant her mantra with every step she took, and visualize anyone who came to speak to her as her cherished deity. She saw all of nature, both sentient and insentient, as God, and thus loved and served them.

Amma says that devotion is not confined to the prayer room or to ritual acts like circumambulating the temple shrine. Real devotion is the compassion that we show others. This outward flow of compassion cleanses and purifies our heart. This is why Amma gives us many opportunities to serve others selflessly. Selfless actions attract divine grace and allow us to forget ourselves. Compassion is the yardstick by which we can measure our closeness to God. Amma says that spirituality begins and ends with compassion. To think that the ego will disappear if we just sit still with our eyes closed is a misconception. Amma's prescription for the present age—a combination of *bhakti* (devotion), *karma* (selfless action) and *jnana* (spiritual knowledge)—can heal all our spiritual maladies.

True love for the Guru is obedience to her teachings. Adi Shankaracarya, the foremost exponent of Advaita, the philosophy of non-duality, was able to mold the illiterate Giri into Totakacarya, a saint and scholar, because of the disciple's total obedience and humble dedication to his Guru. Knowledge dawns within the heart of a disciple who has complete surrender.

Hanuman was able to leap across the ocean and console Sita because of his unswerving faith in Lord Rama.

How can an ordinary person gain devotion? According to the *Narada Bhakti Sutra*, '*mukhyatastu mahatkripayaiva bhagavad kripaleshad va*'—'By the grace of great souls or through a little of divine grace' (38).

I grew up with devotion to God but had no knowledge about the real nature of devotion. Before meeting Amma, I used to spend much of my time in the Sri Mahadeva Temple, dedicated to Lord Shiva. I would wake up to the call of the temple conch in the wee hours of the morning, and would spend my evenings in listening to and singing bhajans. I built up a rapport with the Lord and shared with him all my joys and sorrows. Let me recount an incident that gave me a small experience of divine energy.

I was the top student for my first- and second-year Bachelor of Science (B.Sc.) degree. Overambitious, I was bent on being the top student in my third year also. I spent five sleepless days and nights studying before the examinations. But during the exam, I could not recollect what I had learned. This was a big shock for me. I sat for the same exams again later, and this time, scored high marks.

I applied to six colleges in Calicut to pursue a Master's degree. All my friends who had applied to these colleges were invited to attend interviews. I did not hear from any. I became impatient with Lord Shiva and told him, "I don't want you! From now on, I'm going to pray to Lord Krishna!"

For the first time in my life, I started chanting "Krishna... Krishna..." with every breath I took. Four or five days passed this way. One afternoon, I was lying on my mat and chanting. Although my eyes were closed, I was very alert and aware.

Suddenly a voice resounded within, around and above me. It filled the atmosphere and suffused my body like the brilliant rays of the sun. The voice said, "Do not worry. You will receive notifications from five colleges."

This announcement was followed by a deep silence. I jumped up and looked around. There was no one. That voice calmed my mind, assuaged my heart, and infused me with self-confidence. True enough, I received invitations for interviews from five colleges.

A few months after this incident, I heard that an 'Amma' was coming to the temple. From that moment onwards until I met Amma in person, my heart was filled with a joy that I had never experienced before. The temple committee entrusted me with the job of holding a lighted lamp in front of Amma. As I stood in front of the sanctum sanctorum with the lamp in my hands, Amma entered and stood in front of me. As everyone prostrated before her, I gazed at her in stunned silence. At that time, I did not realize that she was the source of the bliss that I was constantly experiencing, and that after six years, I was going to spend the rest of my life with her. It was only after I heard Amma speak that I understood whose disembodied voice I had heard earlier. The way she called me "darling daughter" seemed so familiar to me.

Amma initiated me with a mantra. When she left, I returned home and burst into tears. My heart seemed empty. It was then that the desire to live with Amma sprouted in my heart. I went to Amritapuri for Amma's birthday. Reaching here, I felt that it was home. As I listened to Amma's bhajans, tears streamed down my cheeks. I prayed for her blessings before returning home.

But obstacles came one after another, and I did not know that these obstacles were leading me to Amma. I started chanting

"Amma... Amma..." continuously with the conviction that she was the Mother of the Universe.

One night, I had a dream darshan of Amma. She spoke to me about the trifling nature of the world and told me to take refuge at her holy feet. Though it was a dream, yet it wasn't. It was a true vision, because I woke up a new person, my attitude totally different from that of the girl who had gone to sleep. These dream visitations recurred for many days and Amma clarified all my doubts in the dreams. I gave her my word that my life was hers, to be spent in her service. During these dream darshans, Amma bolstered my self-confidence and calmed my heart. Thus, Amma, who takes all of us across the ocean of *samsara* (repeated births and deaths), began severing my ties to the world.

I somehow convinced my family members to allow me to go and see Amma once more, and went to Amritapuri. But Amma did not show any sign of recognizing me. When I asked Amma if I could stay here, she said, "I'll tell you later."

After I returned home, I abandoned all my temple-centered routines and began to concentrate wholly on ashram activities. I started chanting more mantras in a bid to join the ashram sooner. Finally, on April 15th, 1996, the day of *Vishu*, Amma granted me refuge at her holy abode.

I had dedicated my life to Amma and pledged to serve her. She gave me many opportunities to develop surrender and to weaken my latent tendencies by sending me to the Kodungallur Amrita Vidyalayam (AV) after just three months in the ashram.

Before joining the ashram, I had sat for an entrance exam that would permit me to work as a researcher in the Central Marine Fisheries Research Institute (CMFRI). Six months after joining AV, I received a phone call from home, informing me that CMFRI had sent a letter asking me to attend an interview. As the central government job was highly coveted, my family members insisted that I should try to secure it. One of my brothers even bought an emergency flight ticket so that he could pick me up from Kodungalloor and take me back home. But on the day my brother was supposed to fly, a nation-wide air strike was announced. Amma thus saved me.

In 2007, Amma asked me to take charge of Thalassery AV. Receiving such opportunities is a sign of the Guru's grace and a test from her. As long as we do our best, we will receive 'grace marks' from the Guru. Even if we do not pass the test, we can learn a lot from failure. However, if we try to dodge the test, such opportunities may not arise again. Divine grace flows unceasingly to the disciple who obeys the Guru.

In 2016, Thalassery AV applied for a grant of 20 *lakh* (two million) rupees to set up a research laboratory, named 'Atal Tinkering Lab,' for the school children. We were shortlisted for the grant and asked to present our proposal at Osmania University, Hyderabad. Amma was in Europe then, and Dr. Maneesha[9] conveyed the news to her.

Amma personally oversaw this project. We sent her many topics, which the children proposed; with great hesitation, I also added my proposal for a water project. Amma selected the water project. Long before I joined the ashram, I had prayed to Lord Krishna to make me a scientist. The Lord had now taken it upon herself to guide me through each step of the project.

---

[9] Director & Professor at Amrita Center for Wireless Networks and Applications and Dean of International Programs, Amrita Vishwa Vidyapeetham (Amrita University).

Every day, Dr. Maneesha would email me instructions from Amma. She gave clear instructions on how to proceed. I was to go to the nearest colony of the poor to collect water samples, which were sent to government labs. I learned about the different kinds of pollutants that contaminate water and about the water-borne diseases caused by drinking such water. I had to test the alkalinity and acidity levels in the water. Amma then asked me to collect water from a more distant water source and to do a comparative study. Just before I left for the presentation, Amma sent a message asking me to bring the water samples in bottles; otherwise, we might not be selected, she said. All the posters we had prepared were shown to Amma for her blessings. I had to prepare PowerPoint slides and train the students on making the presentation. Amma asked Dr. Raghuram of Amrita University to accompany the students for the presentation.

The presentation was on November 6, 2016. On December 2, 2016, the national newspapers published the names of the schools selected to be a part of the 'Atal Tinkering Labs.' Among the schools in Kerala that were selected, Thalassery AV was first in the list.

I hold this lab to be Amma's very own. Students are being trained to do research in Science, Math, Engineering, Technology, Robotics and Artificial Intelligence, among other subjects. Amma asked me to guide them on writing and publishing research papers based on findings from this lab. This has led to the publication of five research papers so far. Two more research publications are being prepared.

We received the first prize in the 2018 Robotics Championship. We also received an opportunity to travel to Thailand and demonstrate our project before an international audience. In

2019, we received First Prize in the National Science Olympiad. In 2021, we received the award for Best Performance in the field of scientific research.

'NITI Aayog,' a public policy think tank of the Indian government, conducts national-level competitions every year on the best student discoveries. In the 2021 'Atal Tinkering Marathon,' Thalassery AV was ranked seventh, thus becoming one among the top 10 schools in India. The children received an opportunity to receive the award from the President of India and to interact personally with him.

I badly wanted this lab to be recognized as one among the best in India. Amma materialized this dream recently when we received the third prize in 'Waterwise,' a competition organized by UNESCO for school children on the importance of water.

The great strides made by the lab must have sown the seed of pride in me. Perhaps, unbeknownst to me, the vainglorious notion that I was a great devotee was also lurking in my subconscious. Amma acted swiftly to get rid of my pride. The Guru does so only to take the disciple to the exalted state of humility. A true disciple will understand that all that the Guru does is for her growth. Only those who have true devotion to the Guru can pass the many tests and enter the Guru's heart.

Let me share an experience that cut my ego down to size. Every time I returned to Amritapuri from Thalassery, I used to spend time sitting next to Amma. But her love and compassion brought out my pride and selfishness. Once, when I brought the 12th-grade students for Amma's darshan, I asked Amma if they could have a photo taken with her. At first, she refused. Later, Amma relented. The initial refusal wounded my ego, and my attachment to the students clouded my good sense. I forgot that whatever Amma does is only for our good. I decided to stay away from her physical presence for a few days and concentrate on the inner Amma instead.

After a few days of sulking, I tried to go near her and talk to her, but she remained aloof. I felt guilty and upset, reflecting on how my own attitude had estranged me from her. I began longing for a smile and a loving word from her. Whenever I tried talking to her, Amma would speak only to the point. I felt that she was pushing me to turn inwards and awaken the awareness of my true self. Finally, I decided to atone for the mistake of being needlessly upset with her and to stop longing for her outward attention. I took an oath to serve her silently with patience, surrender and devotion.

It was around this time that we took the students of Koilandy AV for a two-day excursion to Mysore. We started early in the morning and reached the Kerala-Karnataka border check post at 9:30 a.m. Everyone alighted from the bus. While the driver and teachers submitted the required documents at the check-post office, the children went to the toilet. The next leg of the journey was a two-hour drive through a dense forest filled with wild animals. I looked up at the tall trees and the blue sky and heaved a deep sigh, feeling forlorn. On a sudden impulse, I decided to check my phone for messages. There was one from Swamini Matrupriya: she had sent Amma's audio message from Europe. Amma said, "Amma wants to be with her children in the middle of a forest. She wants to listen to the gurgle of the river, to the songs of the birds. She wants to enjoy the sight of the trees swaying in the wind, and stand beside a waterfall. I imagine myself with you, dancing in joy. I will sit with my children and listen to the sounds of the waterfall, and look at the waves dancing in the river and the trees waving in the wind."

I could not believe it! To receive such an unexpected message, that, too, as we traveled through the forest… I felt my heart being elevated into a state of bliss. Each tree that rose into the sky seemed to be a manifestation of my Mother. My mind soared and touched the white clouds. It reveled in the gurgling streams. Bird song was melody to my ears. I felt Amma smiling at me through the wild flowers. The gentle breeze that wafted floral fragrances filled my heart with the ineffable joy of Amma's presence. Caressing me, she seemed to say, "Look, darling daughter, you're not alone. This universe and the beauty of Nature is your Mother."

Throughout the excursion, I experienced Amma's divine presence. I felt an inner awakening that transformed me. Amma showed me that she is present in all beings, sentient and insentient. She also graciously showed me that pure love is the humble realization that we are even more insignificant than a grain of sand.

Amma says, "Children, love should be for the sake of love only. Then God and the devotee will become one. Such love can only give. Seeing Amma in everything and doing selfless service as an instrument in her hands will erase the feeling of 'I' and 'mine.'"

In *Amritadhara*, a poetic rendition of Amma's teachings, she says,

> Children, if you desire liberation
> renounce selfishness and
> listen to the cries of the suffering.

In this way, we can realize the truth behind the scriptural dictum, *'Tyagenaike amritatvamanushuh'* ('Through renunciation alone can we attain immortality').

Love becomes pure in the silence of surrender. In this state, one has no desire. Amma tells us that we love her truly only when our compassion flows towards everyone.

Once, Lord Krishna was waiting for Radha in Vrindavan. Nature's ethereal beauty was reflected in his face, which was as radiant as the full moon. Radha came with a lovely garland of wild flowers and a pot of fresh butter for the Lord.

Krishna gently reminded her: "Even more than the flowers, I love the tears of compassion that you shed for the suffering of others. When the hands that gather flowers for me serve others, I love them even more. My love flows toward you when your ears listen not just to the melody of my flute, but also to the cries of others. When you console them, my grace gushes towards you. I love you more when you speak sweet and kind words to others than when you sing hymns in my glory. When you see me in everyone and praise their goodness, I love you even more. My hunger will be satiated and my heart will become full when you share this butter with those who are hungry."

Truly, the hearts of the compassionate resound with the mantra *'Lokah samastah sukhino bhavantu'* ('May all beings everywhere be happy and peaceful').

Amma's presence in our lives is *satsang* (company of the holy), which leads to *nissangatva* (detachment), which brings about *nirmohatva* (freedom from delusion), which ushers in *nishcalatatva* (abidance in stillness), which paves the way to *jivan-mukti* (spiritual liberation). This is how Amma leads us to her world of bliss.

Amma is teaching us the dharma appropriate to the times. The situations she creates become intense experiences that remove the *vasanas* (latent tendencies) we have accumulated over many lifetimes. Knowledge dawns in the mind that has been cleansed of all ignorance.

I have nothing but tears of joy to offer Amma for the inner transformation she has brought about in me. May she bless us with Advaita, the non-dual experience of existence, and bestow on us genuine humility. May we all be able to absorb the teachings of Amma, the very embodiment of love, and lovingly serve the world as her humble emissaries.

# 15

# Who is Amma?
*Br. Sthitaprajnamrita Chaitanya*

The *Narada Bhakti Sutras* declare that the nature of love is inexpressible: *'anirvacaniyam premasvarupam'* (51). Just as one who is mute cannot express what he tastes— *'mukasvadanavat'* (52)—the experience of Amma's love is beyond words. In fact, language cannot adequately capture any spiritual experience, which transcends the senses.

Amma is pure experience. Different people have different experiences with her, depending on their level of inner purity. According to the *Sri Lalita Sahasranama* (1,000 names of the Goddess), the Divine Mother is *'antar-mukha-samaradhya'* (870)—to be worshipped mentally—and *'bahir-mukha-sudur-labha'* (871)—difficult to attain for those whose attention is extroverted. Trying to find the Divine Mother outside would be as foolish as looking for fish on trees. To find her within, we must first empty the mind of everything else.

We live in an age that gives utmost importance to intelligence and logic. To illustrate the difference between the heart and the intellect, Amma tells the story of a woman who wrote a poem about her child. She described the child's face as moon-like and compared his eyes to lotus petals. Each of his features was compared to something beautiful. Her husband, a scientist, asked, "What have you written? That his face is like a moon? There are only boulders and craters on the moon!" The husband's rational outlook was in stark contrast to his wife's poetic sensibility.

Amma often says, "Children, God dwells in our heart but we are not there; our attention is on external objects." Owing to this lack of Self-knowledge, we fail to recognize divinity. In the *Bhagavad Gita*, Lord Krishna says,

> *avajananti mam mudha manushim tanum ashritam*
> *param bhavam ajananto mama bhuta-maheshvaram*
>
> When I assume a human guise, the dim-witted disregard me. They do not recognize my divine nature as the sovereign Lord of all beings. (9.11)

The *Bhagavad Gita* declares that whenever *dharma* (righteousness) wanes and *adharma* (unrighteousness) flourishes, God incarnates on earth. In truth, He is all-pervading. When we say that He incarnates, what we mean is that His subtle form becomes manifest. Amma is the manifest form of Parashakti, the supreme power.

Many spiritual masters have been born in India. The Sanskrit name of India is Bharat, which means 'land of light.' *'Bha'* means 'light' (of Self-knowledge) and *'rat'* denotes reveling. One who revels in this light attains unending bliss, the ultimate goal of human life. To reach this state, one needs a Self-realized Guru.

Amma knows that many people are ignorant about spiritual principles. We do not realize that alternating waves of pain and pleasure buffet the shore of life. We do not understand that thoughts and emotions are passing clouds in the clear sky of consciousness. When we suffer, all we want is a shoulder to lean on and someone to wipe away our tears; someone who will listen

## A Recounting of Precious Moments with Amma

to us and share our griefs and joys. This is what Amma is doing, and it is the need of the hour. The change that Amma brings about through just one embrace is hard to describe.

I first saw Amma in 1985 when she came near my family's ancestral temple in Ernakulam. When I heard Amma singing, I forgot myself. I still remember her singing bhajans like *'Sadguro pahimam'* and *'Kannunir kondu.'* The sight of Amma calling out "Amma! Amma!" and laughing ecstatically while singing, captured my heart. After the bhajans, Swamiji (Swami Amritaswarupananda) presented a *Hari-katha*. When darshan started, the program organizer told me, "This is the very Kali whom Sri Ramakrishna worshipped." I joined the queue and had my first darshan.

Later, there was a week-long retreat for members of Yuva Dharmadhara, the youth wing of the Mata Amritanandamayi Math, in Ernakulam. Amma arrived on the last day of the retreat. When she was about to get into the car after darshan, Br. Mulkraj (now Swami Vedamritananda) pointed me out to her. She spoke to me for a few minutes. I don't remember everything she said. However, I do remember what she said about *seva* (selfless service). Amma said that one's service must be firmly rooted in spiritual practices, and that one should serve the world with the same devotion and enthusiasm with which one would serve Amma. She said that serving the world selflessly is true worship. Amma also said one cannot realize God without sacrifice. To succeed in anything, sacrifice is necessary.

I joined the ashram in 1994 and soon started attending Swami Amritageetananda's scriptural classes. In those days, there would be a 20-minute satsang delivered by an ashram resident right after the evening bhajans. At times, Amma would also come to listen to the talk. When I asked Swami Amritageetananda what I should speak on, he said that I was free to choose my own topic. I asked Amma, who said that she would get me married to Miss World and that I should talk about that! After contemplating what Amma said, I understood that in her world, there is only beauty, and the most beautiful thing is one's Self. To attain it, one must forget all other beauties.

What should one do to attain that ultimate beauty? The *Bhagavad Gita* provides an answer:

> *tad-viddhi pranipatena pariprashnena sevaya*
> *upadekshyanti te jnanam jnaninas-tattva-darshinah*

> By humbly submitting to the wise, by asking them questions, and by serving them, they, who have realized the Truth, will impart wisdom to you. (4.34)

Amma wants all of us to experience bliss, which is our very nature. To enjoy it, one must have inner purity. Selfless service helps us gain that inner purity. That is why Amma encourages everyone to do seva. In doing so, she is helping us overcome the obstacles on our path.

The main obstacle is our own ego. To those who are strong enough to withstand her disciplining, Amma will be tough. She has a whole arsenal of weapons to deal with the egos of her children. On several occasions, Amma has remarked, "It is said that after killing Hiranyakashipu, Lord Narasimha calmed down when he saw Prahlada." Then, pointing at me, she would say, "I don't know why it is that whenever I see him, my blood starts boiling! The Kali in me awakens and I give him a resounding scolding!"

I have always considered each one of her scoldings blessings in disguise and receive them all with gratitude.

It is said that the thought of 'I' and 'mine' is an obstacle in the spiritual path. It is not easy to overcome this identification with the body and mind even here in the ashram. For example, I find it hard to get rid of the attitude that 'I'm a senior brahmachari.' In truth, an ashram is like a hospital that treats *'bhava roga'*—the disease of transmigration (cycle of life and death). No one in a hospital will feel proud about being a senior patient. A patient wants to be healed and discharged from the hospital as soon as possible.

In this hospital, Amma is the doctor. If we are ready to undergo her treatment, Amma can release us quickly. She reminds us that if we find fault with others, we are wasting our time. Amma wants us to remain established in the Self and to accept everyone as our own. As mentioned in the *Ashtavakra Gita*,

> *na tvam vipradiko varno nashrami nakshagocarah*
> *asango'si nirakaro vishvasakshi sukhi bhava*

> You are not a member of the Brahmin or any other caste. You are not in any of the four stages of life. You are nothing the eyes can see. You are detached, devoid of form, and witness to everything. Therefore, be happy. (1.5)

When one performs spiritual practices, thought waves subside but do not disappear. If we are not vigilant, our tendencies will arise again when circumstances are conducive. The mind must be trained to face all kinds of circumstances. Amma says, "Children, we must have a mind that sees everything as God and that perceives the Self in every situation. Only then can we say that we are strong."

Amma's words convey spiritual knowledge. Generally, in order to learn anything, it is enough to understand the meaning of the words in which the information is couched. But to realize the Self, one must have a pure heart. To know Amma, one should know oneself. As is said in *Amritadhara*,

> You are the 'I' in me
> and I, the 'you' in you.
> They seem different as we can't see.
> We are one; know this to be true.

Amma does not need to entrust us with a big task to lead us to salvation. She may assign us the simplest seva, but that will be enough to wipe out our ego. What matters is how much *shraddha* (attentiveness and faith) we have in our actions. The more shraddha we bring to our actions, the better we can assimilate spiritual teachings.

I first played *tabla* (Indian drums) for Amma when I was in 8th grade. Amma had come to Ernakulam for a program, and for some reason, the person who was supposed to play tabla for her did not come. With the approval of Br. Venu (now Swami Pranavamritananda), who used to play the tabla for Amma, I played for Amma that day. Before doing so, I went to Amma and said, "Amma, I'm going to play the tabla for bhajans." Amma looked at me intently. Br. Amritatma Chaitanya (now Swami Amritaswarupananda), who was standing nearby, added, "Amma, he plays the tabla." Thus, with Amma's blessings, I began my tabla seva.

## A Recounting of Precious Moments with Amma

During a bhajan recording, after watching me tune the tabla with a hammer, Amma loudly announced, "I'm going to tune Shivan (my previous name) in the same way." Looking at me, she warned, "You mustn't run away!"

Just as the hammer is used to tap the tabla until it is tuned to a particular frequency, through various circumstances, Amma is 'tuning' us all so that our lives resound with the melody of sweet harmony.

The Guru knows the disciples' strengths and weaknesses and guides them accordingly. We must strive to obey the Guru and not act according to our whims and fancies. Only then can we make spiritual progress. Amma once told me, "You should be like a puppet, moving wherever you're pulled." Otherwise, even if we are physically close to the Guru, we will not find a place in Amma's heart. If we allow Amma to dwell in our hearts, we will also dwell in hers.

Amma occupies a place in even in the heart of her critics. I would say that her position is higher than that of a world leader; as the *Sri Lalita Sahasranama* puts it, she is *'sri maharajni'*—'the Empress of the Universe' (2).

In his commentary on the *Brahma Sutras*, Adi Shankaracarya marvels at the Creator's ingenuity in creating the universe: *"manasa api acintya racanarupa..."* Truly, the creative genius behind the universe is beyond the ken of any imagination, and Amma is the Mother of this Universe.

According to the *Bhagavad Gita*,

> *yad yad acarati shreshthas-tat-tad-evetaro janah*
> *sa yat pramanam kurute lokas-tad-anuvartate*

> Whatever the greatest people do, masses follow. The world strives to reach the high standards the great ones set. (3.21)

Amma also sets examples that her children can follow. She cleans roads and toilets, and engages in sand and brick seva for construction work. She prostrates to everyone before giving darshan. Whenever she receives anything, she reverently brings it to her forehead in gratitude. Amma has never missed giving darshan. She is the best crisis manager, one who is able to make decisions quickly and who demonstrates impressive resourcefulness. Making the right decision at the right time with courage is an essential quality of a world leader.

But Amma never takes credit for anything. She says, "Everything was possible because of my children's hard work. Amma has been blessed with good children."

What is the difference between Amma and other philanthropists? The latter focus on mitigating poverty by giving food and clothing, among other things. Amma does the same, but she also does something that no one else can do so well: Amma transforms people by instilling love and compassion in their hearts.

Amma says, "In today's world, people experience two types of poverty: the poverty caused by a lack of food, clothing and shelter, and the poverty caused by a lack of love and compassion. Of these two, the second type needs to be considered first—because, if we have love and compassion in our hearts, then we will wholeheartedly serve those who suffer from lack of food, clothing and shelter."

Amma has had a great impact on the spiritual outlook of people. Until a few decades ago, only a select few used to chant the *Sri Lalita Sahasranama*. Thanks to Amma, the chanting of this *Sahasranama* has become popular all over the world. Amma also propagated Vedic rituals among common people and has initiated countless people with a mantra disregarding their caste, creed or gender.

Amma is also reversing the brain drain that India has been facing. After meeting her, many Indians who were working abroad are now returning home. Many academics in Amrita University are from overseas universities. Within a span of 18 years, Amrita has become the top private university in the country.

No ordinary person can do so much in one life. Amma's accomplishments beggar belief. Her devotees include people from all countries and walks of life, from a common fisherman to the inventor of the super computer.

Let me conclude with a story. When Lord Krishna left Vrindavan, all the *gopis* (milkmaids) were very sad. One gopi said, "When Krishna returns, we will not let him go again."

Another said, "When the Lord comes, I will ask for a boon of dancing with him every day!"

Other gopis also aired their aims: "I want to feed Krishna butter every day." "I will ask him to take me with him to Mathura." "I want the opportunity to fan him daily..."

Only Radha did not say anything. Seeing this, the other gopis asked her, "Why are you silent? Don't you want anything from our Lord?"

Radha said, "When a desire comes to mind, I surrender it at the Lord's feet. Krishna's wish is my wish. His happiness is my happiness."

Let us also surrender our desires at Amma's sacred feet and make the effort to attain our goal. We must never forget that we need to put in effort to receive her blessings. May Amma bless us all with the discernment and dispassion to love and serve others with the right attitude.

# 16

# God Never Abandons Her Devotee
*Bri. Hridayamrita Chaitanya*

Sanatana Dharma describes three traditional paths that lead to God-realization: *jnana* (knowledge), *karma* (action) and *bhakti* (devotion). The path of bhakti, or devotion to the deity one likes, is discussed in great depth in the *Bhagavad Gita*.

> *kshipram bhavati dharmatma shashvat-shantim nigacchati*
> *kaunteya pratijanihi na me bhaktah pranashyati*
>
> Quickly attaining a virtuous mind, my devotee becomes ever peaceful. O Arjuna, declare that my devotee will never perish! (9.31)

Regardless of the wrongs done in the past, those who have enshrined God in their heart will surely be transformed. All their sinful traits will vanish, and the Lord assures us that they will attain permanent peace.

How does one become a devotee? The *Srimad Bhagavatam* elucidates the nine forms of devotion through which a devotee can attain God:

1. *shravanam*—hearing the glories of God;
2. *kirtanam*—singing his glories;
3. *smaranam*—remembering the Lord continuously;
4. *pada sevanam*—serving the Lord;

5. *archanam*—worshipping him;
6. *vandanam*—offering him salutations;
7. *dasyam*—developing the attitude of being God's servant;
8. *sakhyam*—developing the attitude of friendship with the Lord; and
9. *atma nivedanam*—surrendering completely to him. (7.5.23)

It is said that when a devotee adopts one of these forms of devotion towards his preferred deity, his heart will gradually be cleansed of impurities.

Lord Krishna declares further:

> *ananyas-cintayanto mam ye janah paryupasate*
> *tesham nityabhiyuktanam yoga-kshemam vahamyaham*
>
> To those who constantly meditate on me and worship me alone, I provide what they lack and preserve what they already have. (9.22)

We can see the relevance of this statement when we look at the life of the great sage, Maharishi Valmiki. The Maharishi was once a cruel bandit, a forest-dweller who killed passers-by to rob them of their belongings. One day, he chanced upon the *Saptarshis*, the seven enlightened sages, who were passing through the forest, and attempted to rob them. Interacting with them, he realized that all his actions had consequences that he would have to suffer alone. He felt deep remorse and surrendered to the sages. Under their tutelage, he started chanting the divine name of Sri Rama continuously and with total dispassion. His concentration and dispassion were so intense that even when a termite hill grew over his still body, he remained unaware of it. In the course of

## A Recounting of Precious Moments with Amma

time, he emerged from his penance an enlightened sage, filled with compassion and empathy.

The same man, when he later saw a hunter kill a crane and its mate dying of shock, was so moved by this pitiful sight that he spontaneously uttered a verse, considered the first verse in Sanskrit literature. This incident testifies to how a sinner had become compassionate through the power of devotion. If the seven sages had refused him spiritual instruction because he was a cruel hunter, Valmiki, the enlightened poet, would never have come into being, nor the *Ramayana*, one of the greatest epics ever.

Amma can likewise effect a transformation in a person through a look, a word or one darshan. Once, the parents in an Indian family living the West told Amma that their daughter was not devoted to Amma or keen on meeting her. Amma told them to bring her for darshan. At first, the girl refused but later relented. Amma gave her a sweet and loving darshan and asked her to sit by her side. The girl did as told, and started watching Amma as she continued giving darshan. She saw Amma wiping away the tears of people and was moved. Before leaving the hall, she bought a photo of Amma. She kept that photo in her bedroom. In a short time, she started taking part in Amma's charitable activities and became an even more active devotee than her parents.

In the *Bhagavatam*, there is a story of a lifeless Kadamba tree that stood on the banks of the Kalindi River. To stop the venomous serpent Kaliya spewing poison into the river, Sri Krishna climbed up the withered tree and jumped into the Kalindi River. It is said that with every step he took, green shoots sprang up on the tree, which became alive again. Similarly, how many withered lives have blossomed by Amma's darshan and touch; how many lives have been transformed!

Like a huge ocean liner, Amma is capable of taking millions across the ocean of *samsara* (cycle of birth and death). Through her life, Amma teaches us how a human being can become divine. She reminds us that human beings are not meant to live like animals—merely eating, sleeping and procreating. She offers opportunities for all of us, regardless of our culture or faith, to remember God in our own way. The spiritual practices that Amma promotes wherever she goes—including *archana*, meditation, scriptural study, selfless service, bhajans and worship—cater to people of all inclinations. Through her example, she inspires us to do our duty to our family and society, become selfless, and do good deeds. Amma's glance, touch and *sankalpa* (spiritual resolve) are all full of divine energy. Any one of these is enough to transform a person.

If I had not met Amma, I would certainly have been drowned by the swirling vortex of samsara, not knowing the goal of life. When I first heard about her, one of my friends cautioned me against going to see her, saying that she was a fraud. I decided not to see her. Amma's program was held at a Shiva temple near my ancestral home. My late cousin, Bri. Bhavamrita Chaitanya, was a great influence in my life and instrumental in bringing me to Amma. When Bhavamritaji heard that Amma was coming, she became excited even though she had never heard of Amma before; perhaps it was a past-life connection.

Both of us attended Amma's program. Bhavamritaji was so moved that she was crying throughout the bhajans. When I asked her why she was crying, she remained silent. When Amma began to give darshan, Bhavamritaji joined the queue immediately. As for me, although I liked the bhajans, I did not want to go near

Amma. Finally, someone forcibly put me into the darshan line, and that is how I went for my first darshan.

When Amma hugged me, I felt as if a form of Devi (the Goddess) as huge as the Himalayas was hugging me, and that I was just a tiny babe on her shoulder. In that moment, I knew beyond any doubt that Amma was not an ordinary being; she was divine. I felt a great peace descending upon me. Amma smiled and let me go. It was a wondrous minute.

The change that Amma brought about in me has been tremendous. From not wanting to go near her, I long to be in her physical presence so much that Amma has to constantly say, "Chitra (my old name)! Get up! Go! Always sitting near me!" Who can resist that divine magnet?

Bhavamritaji and I were from a joint family. In Kerala, it was customary for joint families—parents, grandparents, uncles and aunts, siblings and cousins—to live under one roof. After meeting Amma, we started waking up before dawn daily to do the archana and to sing bhajans for two hours at dusk, just as they do in the ashram.

Once, one of our visiting uncles got annoyed with our loud chanting early in the morning, as it was disturbing his sleep. He said, "You girls ought to be locked up in a room!" We were hurt by his angry words and lowered the volume of our chanting. That very evening, this uncle quarreled with his wife, who threatened to jump into the well! Our neighbors got involved, separated the two, and locked them up in two different rooms in the house! After this incident, the uncle never complained about our archana again.

Amma often says that the words spoken by a *mahatma* (spiritually illumined soul) will become fulfilled. Such is the power of their spiritual energy. So, when Amma tells us to do something, we must sincerely strive to obey her, for she has only our best interests and spiritual growth in mind.

One day, Amma told me to go to Srayikkadu, a neighboring village, to teach the children there how to play the harmonium; I was to cycle there. I told Amma, "Amma, I don't play the harmonium well enough to teach others." She said, "Label the keys—*Sa, Ri, Ga, Ma…*[10]—and start teaching!" Hearing this, I did not dare to tell her that I did not know how to ride a bicycle. I borrowed a cycle and started practicing riding.

On the designated day of the first harmonium class, I set out for the village on the bicycle. The road was full of potholes and puddles. My mantra chanting flowed like an unbroken river and my prayers to Amma became intense! When I saw a lorry coming from the opposite direction, my heart sank at first. Then, my prayers became even more fervid: "Amma! You sent me to do this work! Now, save me!"

I reached the venue without incident. It was a shelter built for the villagers after the tsunami. When the tsunami victims received their newly built homes, this shelter had been abandoned. When I arrived, I saw the frightening sight of about a dozen street dogs at the door. I reminded myself that Amma, the Divine Mother, had sent me and would look after me. Sure enough, as I neared the entrance, the dogs looked at me and made way for me.

The children arrived and I taught them '*Sa, Ri, Ga, Ma…*' just as Amma had instructed. While cycling back, I began worrying again: "How long will I have to ply this dismal road? Why did Amma give me this work?" I feverishly began chanting my mantra again. Perhaps Amma had given me this *seva* (selfless service) to

---

[10] The Indian *svaras* or notes; the equivalent of the Western solfege (Do, Re, Mi…)

## A Recounting of Precious Moments with Amma

teach me how to do mantra japa with undivided focus. Once I sat on the bicycle, I would not turn my head left or right out of fear, but look only straight in front of me, like a blinkered horse. Amma often says that in the spiritual life, we ought to be like such a horse, not distracted by the sights on either side of the road. Perhaps, this was her way of driving home this lesson to me.

After a few days, I heard some good news: the entire road, from the ashram to the village, was to be repaved, as a cabinet minister was expected to visit a nearby village soon. Within days, the road I took became smoothly paved. I believe that if we follow Amma's instructions sincerely, the universe will remove all the obstacles on our path.

After joining the ashram, I became passionate about singing bhajans. Amma also encouraged me with sweet comments like, "Hearing you sing, Amma feels that she has received wings to fly!" The truth is, it is by Amma's grace alone that our budding talents have blossomed.

Once, a senior brahmacharini was asked to draw up a list of brahmacharinis who could sing. My name was not included. When I innocently asked her why my name was not on the list, she curtly replied, "You don't need to sing!" Hurt, I walked away and cried. I resolved that I would never again desire to sing. I felt that this was God's will. Two days later, someone told me that Amma was calling me. When I went to Amma, she said, "Chitra, when Amma is giving darshan, you should sit in front and sing!" Amma had known how hurt I had been. She alone loves us sincerely. Since then, by Amma's grace, brahmacharinis have been singing one-and-a-half hours in front of Amma during darshan.

One of the bhajans that Amma sings, *'Katinnu Katayi,'* begins thus:

*katinnu katayi manassin manassay*
*kanninnu kannayi vilasunnoramme*

O Mother, who shines as the ear of the ear, mind of the mind, and eye of the eye...

Truly, Amma knows all that we see, hear or think, because she dwells within us as our very self. Wherever we are in the world, it is enough if we are tuned to Amma. This is the only way we can know and experience her. We must be truthful and sincere with Amma. If we are, her grace will always be with us.

In the *Bhagavad Gita*, Sri Krishna guarantees that one who has completely surrendered everything to God will attain him (18.66). May we, Amma's children, be able to do all our work with an attitude of self-surrender, have the deepest devotion to Amma, live with the aim of becoming one with her, and eventually merge into Amma.

# 17

# Karma Yogini
*Bri. Abhijnanamrita Chaitanya*

Lord Krishna says,

> *buddhiyukto jahatiha ubhe sukrta dushkrte*
> *tasmad yogaya yujyasva yogah karmasu kaushalam*
>
> Endowed with the wisdom of even-mindedness, one abandons both good and evil deeds. Therefore, dedicate yourself to yoga. Yoga is skill in action. (*Bhagavad Gita*, 2.50)

Only one whose mind is steady and discerning, and who does his or her duty without thinking about reward or punishment can act with even-mindedness. Lord Krishna says that such skill in action is karma yoga.

People tend to believe that being skillful means being able to execute a task flawlessly, but karma yoga is not technical proficiency. Karma yoga entails renouncing the fruits of actions. No doubt, doing selfless deeds is meritorious. However, a karma yogi is not concerned with *punya* (spiritual merit) or *paapa* (sin), only in dedicating all actions to God. Such an attitude purifies the mind and makes it equanimous.

Avatars and Self-realized beings, who perceive the Self in all, demonstrate perfect equanimity. The scriptures say, '*Sarvam devimayam jagat'* — 'the Divine pervades the whole universe.' We must try to convince ourselves of this idea by constantly reflecting on it. When this idea sinks in, we will see the world differently. *Mahatmas* (spiritually illumined souls) remain centered in the Self in all situations. Amma smiles with us, plays with us, and even scolds us, but none of these affect her inwardly. All her actions serve only to help us move closer towards purity. Such is Amma's boundless compassion.

When the tsunami struck the South Indian coast in 2004, Amma was giving darshan in the Kali Temple. The first sign of the impending disaster was a huge wave that lapped the ashram grounds. At that, Amma issued instructions to summon back all those who were at the beach. Soon after that, the deluge swamped the ashram, with the water level reaching four feet. An ordinary person would have panicked, but Amma took control of the situation. She stopped darshan, came down from the Kali Temple, waded through the water to the main gate, and initiated relief measures. She took steps to shift the villagers and ashram residents across the backwaters. She made provisions for the villagers to receive basic necessities — food, clothing and temporary shelter. In a short period, the ashram also built houses for those who had lost theirs in the tsunami. Amma's response clearly revealed her skill and even-mindedness.

More recently, Amma's skill in action was on display in her handling of the coronavirus pandemic. Before the government announced the lockdown, she summoned the ashram residents from around the world back to the safety of Amritapuri, and conducted the auspicious *diksha* ceremony, initiating more than 250 monastics into *sannyasa* and *brahmacharya*, a milestone event in the annals of the ashram. Amma also reached out to people all over the world, and instituted measures to soften the adverse economic, social and emotional impact of the pandemic. Who else but Amma can demonstrate such mastery over situations?

In the *Bhagavad Gita*, Lord Krishna declares:

*na me parthasti kartavyam trishu lokeshu kincana*
*nanavaptam avaptavyam varta eva ca karmani*

O Partha, I have no duty to do in any of the three worlds, and nothing to gain or attain. And yet, I am always engaged in action. (3.22)

The actions of a *mahatma* (spiritually illumined soul) are not motivated by thoughts of gain or duty. They act only to do good and to set an example to others. An incident from the *Mahabharata* is illustrative. Preparations for the *Rajasuya Yajna*, a ritual to elevate a king to an emperor, were underway in the kingdom of Indraprastha. What was Lord Krishna doing? He was washing the feet of the guests! People asked him in consternation why was he doing that, and the Lord replied that as he had not been given any responsibility and seeing that no one had been assigned to receive the guests traditionally by washing their feet, he took that work upon himself. Later, Krishna was seen clearing the leaves from which the guests had eaten food in the dining hall.

Isn't Amma also like that? She is always at the forefront of any task, whether cleaning the septic tank, cutting vegetables, doing sand seva or stitching masks. She does everything with utmost calm and skill.

Amma has said, "I am a sweeper, the sweeper of human minds." She has taken it upon herself to clean human minds and to fill them with love and a zeal for serving others.

Amma says that working without mental purity is like pouring milk into an unclean vessel; the milk will get spoilt.

I am reminded of an incident that happened in school. On *Gandhi Jayanti*, the birthday of Mahatma Gandhi, students from the third grade were divided into three groups headed by three leaders and asked to weed three different areas. After they had finished, I inspected their work. The first group had done impressive work. The second group had removed weeds from here and there. The third group had removed all the weeds but had not cleared them. I commended all the three groups and then pointed out the shortcomings of the work done by the second and third groups.

Similarly, Amma points out the flaws in our work only to help us develop more *shraddha* (attentiveness). When she does so, we also realize that she is watching all our actions and that not even the smallest detail escapes her attention.

Karma yogis must perform only actions that foster mental purity. They must not do anything that pricks their conscience. What is important is not *how much* work we do but *how well* we do it.

In karma yoga, one must have both awareness while working and an attitude of dedication to the work. In order to develop the spirit of dedication, we must cultivate love for and faith in God. We must strive to be like a brush in the hands of the Divine. When we work as an instrument, the work we do will not bind us. To illustrate, we can dissolve milk in water and vice versa, but butter, which is obtained by churning milk, does not dissolve either in milk or water. Work done without any selfish motive but with dedication to God is like butter; it remains detached.

## A Recounting of Precious Moments with Amma

Amma often reminds us that there are three factors that can bring any action to fruition: time, effort and divine grace. It takes time for a plant to bear fruit. Before that, we must sow the seed. Even if we do so and water it, there are forces that can prevent the seed from sprouting. For the seed to sprout, grow and bear fruit, God's grace is also necessary. This also means if we do not get the desired result, we must accept it as the will of God.

I am reminded of an incident. When I was in 10th grade, I could not sit for the board examinations as I had contracted chicken pox. I was quite upset. Expecting that Amma would sympathize with me, I visited Amritapuri with my mother. When I told Amma what had happened, she started laughing loudly. I felt annoyed because I thought that Amma was being insensitive. But when my mother went for darshan and told Amma about my not having been able to sit for the examinations, Amma said, "Isn't your daughter with you now?" We did not understand what Amma meant but left it at that.

After a few days, we consulted an astrologer, who said that I had been going through a particularly malefic period and that "some *shakti* (divine power)" had saved me. That was when it dawned on us that Amma had been protecting me all along. By Amma's grace, I was able to accept what happened as her will and that it had happened for my own well-being.

Amma conveys sublime scriptural principles in simple language so that we can understand them. She says that spiritual teachings are to be put into practice to help us overcome challenges in life, and not to develop our ego. When we interact with others, we can understand how spiritually mature we are by the way our mind reacts.

I am reminded of my own reactions in my early days as a school principal in one of the Amrita Vidyalayams. When a few parents spoke disparagingly about the school, I used to feel righteous anger and retaliate in the same tone. Later, I understood that anger was meaningless, and that it was more productive to listen patiently and try to solve the problem. I was able to overcome such situations because I tried to practice at least some of Amma's teachings.

Life in the ashram gives us golden opportunities to follow the path of karma yoga. The circumstances we encounter may be favorable or otherwise. What matters is how we face them. Amma often reminds us that we have come to spiritual life to reduce or exhaust our karmic burden, not to increase it. Just as some diseases can be treated with medicines, whereas others require surgery, and yet others cannot be cured even with surgery, so, too, some of our karmic burdens can be reduced by penitence and prayer; others may be mitigated by doing *pujas* (ritual worship); yet others must be borne stoically. As all of us have our own karmic burden, let us not forget that having faith in and an attitude of surrender to Amma can give us the strength and stamina to shoulder it.

Being a karma yogi does not mean having expertise in some area. For spiritual seekers, expertise is doing the work that the Guru has assigned them without attachment and with discernment. In other words, working with awareness is the essence of skill in action. In this way, we can try to uphold our *dharma* (duties) and strive to earn Amma's grace.

Often, the ego prevents us from turning our work into a form of worship. I am reminded of how Amma taught me to manage my ego. The school's Annual Day had not been celebrated for two years. I had no intention of conducting it that year either because of various issues. But when teachers and parents kept insisting,

## A Recounting of Precious Moments with Amma

I finally gave in. I prayed fervently to Amma before sending invitations to the guests.

The inaugural program went off without a hitch. After the formal function ended and I had seen the guests off, I sat down in the hall to watch the rest of the program. Even then, I continued praying to Amma for the rest of the function to proceed without a problem.

After a few minutes, a few teachers came to me and expressed what an excellent function it was and said that it had been even better than those of the previous years. Hearing this, I started swelling up with pride and stopped praying to Amma. Then, some parents came to congratulate me on how well-organized the program was. A wave of pride swept over me. I began floating on cloud nine...

Suddenly, the power supply went off, plunging the place into total darkness. I slumped into my chair, like Arjuna had done in his chariot! I could not understand how the electric supply had been cut, as we were using the generator. I started calling out feverishly to Amma again. The electrician came and sorted out the problem. He later told me that there had been a minor problem with the switch. This incident was a good warning to me about what can happen if I forget Amma.

Lord Krishna, who served as Arjuna's charioteer, incarnated to uproot egos and rout *adharma* (unrighteousness). Amma has likewise come to remove our pride and to re-establish *dharma* (righteousness). She is the cause of all auspiciousness, victories and spiritual advancement. We are truly blessed to be with her. Amma is eagerly waiting to impart wisdom and strength to us and thus elevate us spiritually. May we all become deserving of her ample grace. ॐ

# 18

# Karma Yoga
*Br. Srinathamrita Chaitanya*

Karma yoga is performing *karma* (action) with discernment and an attitude of surrender to God. It is doing work without attachment to its outcome. Lord Krishna defines it thus:

> *buddhi-yukto jahatiha ubhe sukrta-dushkrte*
> *tasmad yogaya yujyasva yogah karmasu kaushalam*

> Possessed of wisdom, one gives up both virtue and vice. Therefore, devote yourself to yoga. Yoga is skill in action. (*Bhagavad Gita*, 2.50)

When we work with an attitude of surrender, we are not concerned with gaining merit, only with attaining God.

We can forgo the fruits of our actions by acting with the consciousness that God is the real doer, that we are merely conduits for divine energy, and by constantly remembering God. In this way, we can try to elevate each and every karma so that it becomes karma yoga.

Karma yoga purifies the mind. Having attained mental purity, through devotional practices and the path of Self-inquiry, the seeker becomes a *sthita-prajna*, one who is established in spiritual wisdom. According to Amma, the paths of karma, *bhakti* (devotion) and *jnana* (knowledge) are not separate but interconnected.

She says that devotion and knowledge are like the two sides of a coin. Karma yoga is the seal on the coin, what gives it value.

In Hanuman, we see a perfect blend of all three. He was an indefatigable worker. When he heard the names of Lord Rama, he would weep with devotion. He also possessed remarkable knowledge of the scriptures.

No one can avoid action. Lord Krishna says as much in the *Bhagavad Gita*:

> *na hi kashcit kshanam api jatu tishthatyakarma-krt*
> *karyate hyavashah karma sarvah prakrti-jair gunaih*
>
> No one can remain without doing action for even a moment. Truly, all beings are compelled to act by their innate qualities. (3.5)

Even thinking is action. Amma reminds us that the agitation in human minds affects nature. If we act on our negative thoughts, we must definitely bear the consequences of it. Amma says that our aura captures the subtle form of our karma as *vasanas* (latent tendencies). This means that we can be free from the bondage of karma only when our mind is pure. This is the challenge — purifying the mind so that our work can be a form of worship.

Daksha's *yajna* became a *yuddha* (war) whereas Arjuna's war became a yajna. Daksha was a devotee, had knowledge of the Vedas, and was a great king, but because of his selfishness and pride, his yajna turned into a war. In contrast, Arjuna's attitude of surrender helped him to act without egoism, and thus the Mahabharata War became a yajna.

When we discharge our duties with the feeling that God is acting through us, for the benefit of the world, and without seeking any personal profit, our actions will not accrue any *punya* (merit) or *paapa* (sin). When we dedicate our actions to Amma, constantly thinking of her, our work will become worship. Amma gives us many opportunities to do this.

In the *Bhagavad Gita*, Lord Krishna says:

> *tapamyaham aham varsham nigrhnamyutsrjami ca*
> *amrtam caiva mrtyush ca sad asacchaham arjuna*
>
> O Arjuna, as the sun, I radiate heat. I withhold and release rain. I am both death and immortality. I am both spirit and matter. (9.19)

Nature is constantly teaching us lessons in selflessness. The sun gives energy to the world without expecting anything in return. The sun's rays evaporate sea water. The water vapor forms clouds that, upon condensation, fall as rain, thus nourishing flora and fauna.

Trees produce the oxygen we need. On an average, one human being consumes about 550 liters of pure oxygen a day, which is worth about 13 *lakh* (1.3 million) rupees. We take so much from nature. What are we giving back?

Most of the ancient kings of India forsook material pleasures at some point in their lives and dedicated the rest of their lives to performing spiritual practices in forests. The earth is a *karma bhumi*, sphere of action. Instead of acting selfishly all the time, if we can also dedicate some of our actions to the welfare of others, including Mother Nature, we can help to restore the environmental balance. This will also benefit us.

The story of the squirrel in the *Ramayana* is well-known. It wanted to do its bit to help Lord Rama build a bridge across the ocean to Lanka. Moved by its sincere efforts, the Lord picked up the squirrel and affectionately stroked its back. It is said that the three stripes on the back of squirrels were from Lord Rama's strokes. The squirrel's contributions might have been small, but in God's eyes, nothing is insignificant. By marking the squirrel with stripes, Sri Rama proclaimed to the world the greatness of selfless service.

If we get a chance to do a little *seva* (selfless service) for Amma, she will bless us with the three boons of *shraddha*, *bhakti* and *vishvas*—attentiveness, devotion and faith—just as Lord Rama imprinted the three strokes on the squirrel's back as a mark of its sincerity and selflessness.

After the Mahabharata War, Lord Krishna advised Yudhishthira to perform the grand Rajasuya Yajna. At the end of the ceremony, a strange-looking mongoose appeared on the scene and started rolling on the ground. Half its body was golden. Yudhishthira asked him, "Why are you rolling on the ground?"

The mongoose explained. There was once a poor Brahmin who lived with his wife and two children in a village. For days, they did not have any food to eat and were starving. Finally, the father managed to obtain some food by begging. He brought it home and was about to share the food with his wife and children when a guest arrived, saying that he was famished and wanted some food. The poor Brahmin willingly gave his share to the guest. But the guest's hunger was not appeased. He again asked for some more food. The wife offered him her share. Still not satisfied, the guest extended his hand for more food. The son offered his share. The guest's hunger was appeased only after the daughter also offered him her share.

Though the Brahmin family died of starvation, they left their bodies with peaceful minds. The mongoose said, "When I rolled over the ground there, where the remnants of food had fallen, half my body became golden. Since then, I have been searching for another place where such a holy yajna took place so that the other half of my body can also become golden. When I heard about your yajna, I came and rolled over the ground here. Alas, the other half of my body remains brown."

Yudhishthira's pride in his yajna was humbled. The fable of the mongoose illustrates that what really counts is not how much is sacrificed but the love behind the sacrifice. It also glorifies the greatness of a true yajna.

Amma's whole life is a yajna. She is constantly engaged in selfless actions for the benefit of the world. Her every word and act are filled with beauty and wholeness. Just like Sri Rama and Sri Krishna, Amma has come with the epochal mission of re-establishing *dharma* (righteousness) and sustaining Sanatana Dharma. Over the past few decades, she has given darshan to 40 million people. Amma's glory is spreading all over the world. Never in the history of the world has there been an avatar like Amma.

Owing to the merits accumulated over many lifetimes, we are all able to serve Amma in small ways, like the squirrel in the *Ramayana*. Let me share one such experience I had.

I first met Amma in 1988, when she came to a temple in Palakkad. This temple was near my office. I was not interested in attending the program, but on the pamphlet advertising the program, I noticed two quotes from two eminent personalities, for whom I had great respect: Sri Ottur Unni Namboodiripad, the illustrious composer of Amma's *Ashtottaram* (108 attributes), and Sri Madhavji, a renowned Tantric priest and teacher. Both of them spoke highly of Amma. I decided to go and see Amma.

When I heard Amma singing, I was lost! My heart was so touched by the aura of sanctity emanating from Amma that I cried and cried. Soon after that, I became fully immersed in the local satsang activities.

When the construction of the Palakkad ashram began, the engineer, Sri Narendran, told Amma that he needed someone who could supervise the construction work. She referred me to him, even though I had not told Amma that my work was connected with building construction. At that time, I was a government employee, working as an overseer in PWD (Public Works Department).

I soon found myself fully involved in this seva, which included arranging for materials and supervising the construction work. Every morning, I would rush to the office, which was near the ashram construction site, on a bicycle. On most days, my superior would scold me for habitually reporting late for work. I would just listen and not say anything.

A few days passed. One day, the construction workers were on leave, and there was no work at the site. I reached the office early, thinking that I could avoid a scolding from my boss that day. When I reached the office, I saw that no one other than the office attendant had arrived. When I asked him where the others were, he said that everyone was attending the Junior Superintendent's daughter's wedding ceremony. He had invited me also but I had totally forgotten about it.

That day, there was an inspection. Senior officers from Trivandrum came to our office at 10 a.m. to check if the employees were coming to the office on time. When the officers learnt that the staff were attending a marriage ceremony and had not applied for leave, they were furious. They asked the attendant and me to sign the attendance register, and then put a red mark against the names of all the others. They also left a note asking for an explanation for their absence.

Amma thus saved me from official trouble because I had been trying sincerely to serve her. I could only marvel at her divine play.

I have had many such experiences, wherein I could see Amma's divine hands at work. No doubt, Amma's children all over the world have had similar experiences. May she bless us all with the strength to become an instrument in her hands and to be at her service always.

# 19

## Instrument in Her Hands
*Br. Chidanandamrita Chaitanya*

In the *Bhagavad Gita*, Lord Krishna explains to Arjuna the attitude that a disciple ought to have in order to progress on his chosen path and to do his duty. The Lord gave his advice during the Kurukshetra War, when both armies were facing each other. At this juncture, Arjuna tells Lord Krishna, who was his charioteer, "Krishna, I want to survey the army I am going to fight. Please take the chariot to a place where I can see them all arrayed for battle."

The Lord steers the chariot and deliberately halts in front of Drona, Arjuna's teacher, and Bhishma, the patriarch of the Kuru dynasty. Seeing them, Arjuna becomes disturbed. His attachment to them puts him in a state of confusion. He loses the will to fight the battle. Seeing this, Lord Krishna advises Arjuna and tries to motivate him to do his duty. Eventually, Arjuna surrenders his will to the Lord and asks him for guidance. The Lord says,

> *tasmat tvam uttishtha yasho labhasva*
> *jitva shatrun bhunkshva rajyam samrddham*
> *mayaivaite nihatah purvam eva*
> *nimitta-matram bhava savya-sacin*

> Therefore, arise and acquire glory. Conquer your enemies and enjoy a prosperous kingdom. They have already been killed by me. O Arjuna, just be an instrument. (11.33)

Krishna had created the apt situation for Arjuna to get rid of his confusions and to make him do his duty in the battlefield. "Arjuna, just be a tool in my hands," says Krishna.

Is it easy to become an instrument in the hands of the Divine? What qualities are needed for this? First and foremost, we must not be attached to our likes and dislikes. Secondly, we must be free of the delusions of the world. Thirdly, the ego-centric feeling of 'I' ought to disappear, and in its place, we must have complete surrender to God.

Arjuna, the great warrior, was able to do all this. But what about normal people like us? If someone like Arjuna had so much confusion initially, it goes without saying that people today whose senses have been completely engaged by the distractions of modern life would be so much more deluded.

Fortunately, we have Amma with us. I believe that she is an incarnation of the Divine Mother, who sent Lord Rama and Lord Krishna in the *Treta Yuga* and *Dvapara Yuga* respectively to restore dharma, and she has come with the same mission in this *Kali Yuga*.

The *Sri Lalita Sahasranama*, the 1,000 names of the Divine Mother, hails the Divine Mother thus:

> *om karanguli nakhotpanna narayana dashakrtyai namah*

> Salutations to the Divine Mother, who created all ten incarnations of Narayana (Vishnu) from her fingernails. (80).

## A Recounting of Precious Moments with Amma

Why did she have to incarnate on earth? It was to accomplish the difficult task of guiding ordinary people like us to the Truth. When we have such a powerful avatar with us, what should our attitude be? One of Amma's senior disciples once asked Amma what she wanted them to become. Amma took some sand in her hands, gently poured it on the ground, and said, "I want you to become like this sand. People may walk, stand or spit on it, but the sand does not react in any way. Become like this sand."

I used to think that love is a feeling. But after seeing Amma, I realized that love can take a form. She is the very embodiment of love. Once, when Amma was asked about the *karma* (fate, determined by one's actions) of a notorious terrorist, she said, "What that son did was wrong…" I was struck by the extent of her motherly love, for she could refer to even a cruel terrorist as a son. Who other than the Divine Mother can do that? In Amma's opinion, "Even the cruelest killer shows love to his child. So, love is present in him, hidden somewhere in his heart." She has made it her duty to bring out this love from within us.

How is it that Sri Rama, Sri Krishna and Amma are such powerful storehouses of energy? Even nature seems to move according to their wishes. Some say it is by virtue of their oneness with *dharma* (righteousness). Perhaps it is so, but I feel that it is the power of their love, the most powerful weapon. Love can do anything and everything. Lord Rama's weapon was the *kodanda* (bow), and Lord Krishna's, the *sudarshana chakra* (discus), and by these, they annihilated their most deadly enemies. Amma's weapon is love and love alone.

Love has the power to transform even when wielded by ordinary people. Once, there was a school inspection. The 5th grade teacher was a kind woman who loved all her students equally. She did not want any student to look like a dullard before the inspector. She came up with a plan. She told her students, "Children, tomorrow when I ask you questions in front of the inspector, all of you should raise your hands to answer. If you know the answer, raise your right hand. If you don't, raise your left hand. I will pick only the students whose right hands are raised. This will make the inspector think that this is the best class!"

All went well during the inspection. The inspector was happy, but some sixth sense made him suspect that something was amiss. He called on a boy sitting in the last row to stand up. Turning to the teacher, he said, "This boy raised his hand for every question you asked, but did not get a chance to answer any. Please ask him a question."

The teacher was taken aback. She knew the boy well. Whenever she asked him anything, he always said, "I don't know." She thought for a moment and then asked him, "What is the opposite of 'I know?'"

"I don't know," replied the boy. The inspector smiled and left.

How had the teacher pulled off such a stunt? Out of pure love for her students. If an ordinary schoolteacher could do this, imagine how much energy and intelligence the Divine Mother will possess.

Before joining the ashram, I was a software engineer in the United States. I first entered the joyful world of *seva* (selfless service) when I was at San Ramon, California, Amma's first ashram in the US. A few devotees and I would work late into the night after our regular office hours, creating and testing the software to organize registrations for ashram retreats. It was a blissful time of service.

# A Recounting of Precious Moments with Amma

After joining Amma's ashram, for 15 years, I was involved in organizing Amma's Tamil Nadu Tour. Looking back, I clearly see that whatever my health condition was at the time, the energy to do Amma's work always materialized somehow. The programs were always a big success. Later, I understood that everything was happening only by Amma's *sankalpa* (divine resolve). My job was only to be a tool in her hands, acting as if I was working hard, and taking the credit for what Amma did!

Once, a fellow brahmachari went to a village in Tamil Nadu to inform the people there about Amma's upcoming program in a nearby town. Seeing him, one woman appeared to be deeply moved. She approached him and told him earnestly, "Son, I've been yearning deeply to meet this Mother. She has sent you as a messenger!" The brahmachari realized that Amma had sent him to that village to answer that woman's prayer. We are mere instruments in her hands.

When I am not organizing the Tamil Nadu tours, my seva has been teaching in the Amrita School of Engineering in Amrita Vishwa Vidyapeetham (Amrita University). It is a rich and fertile ground for learning and growth, both academic and spiritual.

Once, a student approached me four months before the final examination, asking for additional help in the subject I was teaching. I gave him some instructions, some pointers for self-study, and asked him to approach me whenever needed, to clear his doubts.

Another student approached me one month before the final exam for help. I sent him to a junior teacher to help him personally every day.

A third student came to me one week before the exam, asking for help. I started him on a crash course of four-hour coaching sessions daily, which I personally conducted.

One student came to me for help the day before the exam. I told him to go for Amma's darshan; it was the only thing I could think of to help him at the eleventh hour. That boy did as he was told.

When the results came out, all four had passed. The point here is to try our best, and then to leave the rest to Amma.

A few years ago, Amrita University organized an international cyber-security conference at its Amritapuri campus. We invited many guests from all over the world. We usually bring our guests to meet Amma, who is also the university's chancellor. Among the guests were some of the brightest minds in the field: scientists, academicians and domain experts. Most of them were meeting Amma for the first time. She spent some time discussing the different security threats and issues in the cyber world. A senior scientist said, "Amma, I'm very happy to meet you. You are such a charming person! I don't see any sign of fear in your eyes. You are always cool and composed. Please tell us: how can we be fearless? All the security measures we implement fail eventually. Please tell us a security technique for remaining fearless."

Amma smiled like a child. She said, "No external arrangement can give us total security. Only with inner security can we attain complete fearlessness. Spiritual practices help us gain that inner security."

Amma embraces everyone without discriminating against anyone. Whether rich or poor, scholar or illiterate, everyone regardless of caste, creed, nationality or race has equal access to Amma. To me, Amma is the towering peak among all the *mahatmas* (spiritually illumined souls) who have walked on earth since time immemorial. We have all yearned for many births to meet such a mother. What we cannot gain at Amma's feet, we will not be able to attain anywhere else. If we can renounce our likes and dislikes and become pure instruments in her hands, our lives will become truly blessed.

# 20

# Skill in Action
*Br. Yoga Chaitanya*

The duty of a warrior is to uphold righteousness, vanquish the unrighteous, and protect the weak. But what if the unrighteous people are the warrior's own relatives and teachers? We hear about people covering up or protecting someone who has done wrong because that person is their friend or relative. This is Arjuna's dilemma. He does not want to incur bad karma by killing his family members, even though he knows that his cousins are unrighteous. He feels that it is better to go unarmed into battle and be killed by them. He declares that Bhishma, his grandfather, and Dronacarya, his teacher, are worthy of worship, and does not want to stain his hands with their blood. He feels it is better to beg for alms than to gain a prosperous kingdom at the expense of their lives.

Lord Krishna allays Arjuna's anxiety with the following words:

> *buddhi-yukto jahatiha ubhe sukrta-dushkrte*
> *tasmad yogaya yujyasva yogah karmasu kaushalam*

> Possessed of wisdom, one gives up both virtue and vice. Therefore, devote yourself to yoga. Yoga is skill in action. (2.50)

Usually, when we hear the word 'yoga,' we think of yoga *asanas* or postures. The word 'yoga' comes from the root verb '*yuj,*' which means 'to yoke' a bull, for example, to a bullock cart. Hence, yoga means yoking our individuality to the all-pervading Brahman, the Supreme.

In the verse just quoted, Lord Krishna is referring specifically to karma yoga, the path of becoming one with God through dedicated *karma* (action). Krishna also uses the word 'kaushalam' in association with karma. According to Adi Shankaracarya, kaushalam refers to the ability to act in such a way that its good or bad effects do not bind us. Typically, every action, whether *sukrta* (virtuous action) or *dushkrta* (evil action), results in *punya* or *paapa*, merit or demerit, which we must experience sooner or later. This chain of action and result perpetuates the cycle of birth and death. However, by doing an action with evenness of mind and dedicating it to God, we can rise above the consequences of karma. In this way, we can outwit the stars (change our destiny) and break the wheel of karma, which causes birth and death. This is what Lord Krishna means when he talks about karma yoga, skill in action.

However, what we usually understand by skill in action is proficiency. But according to Adi Shankaracarya, this is not what kaushalam means, although technical proficiency is a byproduct of karma yoga. To illustrate, take the case of athletes.

Many athletes experience a phenomenon called 'being in the zone,' a mental state that enables them to perform to the best of their ability. Their focus is so intense that it leads to a vivid clarity, a sense of ecstasy, and an intuitive understanding of what exactly needs to be done. They forget themselves and feel that they are a part of something larger. In that state, time seems to stand still.

We see this exalted level of proficiency in Amma all the time. How else can she manage all the humanitarian projects, schools, colleges and hospitals with such ease? How else can she oversee the disaster management works in such a timely and efficient manner? On top of all that, Amma meets, counsels and consoles hundreds of thousands of devotees and disciples. Parents find it difficult to manage just two children, but Amma looks after millions. She is not just a *sthita-prajna*, a person established in the highest wisdom, mentioned in the *Gita*. If we have to compare Amma to anyone, it would be to Lord Krishna.

The Lord says that if we perform actions with equanimity and God-centered consciousness, our mind will be cleansed of the impurities of desire, anger, greed, delusion, pride and envy. Such a pure and concentrated mind can contemplate one's true nature. One who has realized his true nature has no sense of 'I'—the sense of being a doer. When there is no ego, karma will not bind. If Arjuna acts without the sense of doer-ship, there is no question of incurring sin by killing family members and teachers.

In the verse quoted earlier, Lord Krishna uses the word *'iha'* (jahati-iha), meaning 'in this life.' He is saying that we can gain both freedom from karma as well as knowledge of our true nature in this very life and thus enjoy *amrita*, the nectar of immortality. Amma has said that true seekers can attain Self-realization in three to four years, provided they follow her instructions to the letter.

Krishna also says *'buddhi-yuktah,'* meaning endowed with wisdom. He explains what this really means two verses earlier:

> *yoga-sthah kuru karmani sangam tyaktva dhananjaya*
> *siddhy-asiddhyoh samo bhutva samatvam yoga ucyate*

> Be steadfast in yoga, O Arjuna. Perform your duty and abandon all attachment to success or failure. Such evenness of mind is called yoga. (2.48)

What does it mean to abandon attachment (*sangam tyaktva*)? Lord Krishna explains it in the previous verse:

> *karmany-evadhikaras te ma phaleshu kadacana*
> *ma karma-phala-hetur bhur ma te sango'stvakarmani*
>
> Your right is to the work only and never to the fruits of it. Let not the results of action be your motive. Do not be attached to inaction either. (2.47)

Amma says three factors are needed to bring any action to fruition: time, effort and grace. Effort alone is not enough. Amma says the next moment is not in our hands. So why worry about the outcome of our effort? Let us surrender it to the Divine. If we can maintain this attitude of detachment, we will be able to do our duty under all circumstances.

Attachment prevents us from acting skillfully. Amma cites the example of a surgeon who is unable to operate on his own child because of attachment. This was Arjuna's problem. He was unable to do his duty because he was attached to his near and dear ones.

It is better to do our duty than to neglect it. But while doing it, we must remember to do our duty for the sake of duty and to dedicate our efforts to God or the Guru. This will give us equanimity and we will cease to worry about success or failure. If we drop all expectations and remain detached from the outcome of our efforts, we will gain freedom from the bondage of karma. This is karma yoga.

A prisoner who misbehaves while serving time will have to serve his full term in prison, whereas one who behaves well will get early parole. Similarly, by working for God, we also can get early parole from the cycle of birth and death.

In 2010, Swamiji (Swami Amritaswarupananda) asked me to take up the Amrita Books publication seva. At that time, ashram publications were not available in bookshops outside. Swamiji took me to Amma to get her permission. She agreed. I was thrilled and excited to get an opportunity to do this important work of spreading Amma's message to the masses. I had many ideas about how to do this seva and many expectations, too. I built many castles in the sky. I imagined that I would get more personal time with Amma. Maybe, she would even call me to her room for meetings!

Reality proved to be different. The next year, during Amma's Indian tours, I met publishers across India. Many said that they were ready to distribute our books, but when I called them later, they made excuses: "Let's wait until the next financial year." I wondered why they would want to lie about being interested. I met many such obstacles.

I also wanted to start an online portal to sell Amma's books, but this plan also ran into many problems. Those meetings with Amma in her room never transpired. I became frustrated and dejected. This situation persisted for a few years.

Then I started studying the *Bhagavad Gita* more deeply and realized that my reactions were diametrically opposite to Lord Krishna's teachings on karma yoga. I was not even-minded in success and failure. I was attached to the results of my work. These insights were an eye-opener. It completely changed my attitude towards seva.

## A Recounting of Precious Moments with Amma

Many of us do seva, but do we act in the spirit of karma yoga? Only when we apply the principles of karma yoga does it truly become seva. Studying the *Gita* helped me tide over a bad time in my life, when, for various reasons, I could not get things done. Amma places great emphasis on the scriptures and had on numerous occasions advised me to study them. Then I understood why. Nothing or no one created the problems. It was my own mind, with its expectations and desires, that created the problems. The mind can be our best friend or our worst enemy.

Karma yoga is nothing but becoming an instrument in God's hands. It means working without the interference of the ego, which is nothing but a bundle of likes and dislikes. Through karma yoga, our likes and dislikes, attractions and aversions slowly get effaced. The mind becomes still, we become a fitting instrument in the Guru's hands, and knowledge of the Self dawns within.

Amma says, "Become like a paint brush in the hands of the painter." In the bhajan *Icchamayi*, the poet declares, "I am an instrument; you are the user. I am a chariot; you are the charioteer; I am the house; you are its owner." In the *Bhagavad Gita*, Lord Krishna says, *"nimitta-matram bhava savya-sacin"* — "O ambidextrous one, be an instrument in my hands" (11.33).

Once, I told Amma that I was not able to meditate because seva in the bookstall was a full-time activity. Amma said that not finding time to meditate was not a problem. She said, "You are like an open pipe connected to the water tank." Amma was implying that the bookstall seva was helping me progress spiritually as I was an instrument doing Amma's work. God's power was flowing freely through me.

Does being an instrument mean becoming a robot or a slave? No. Dedicating one's actions to God is an act of love. When we become an instrument, we experience the love of God. That love motivates us to do our work with dedication and awareness. When we offer our work to God, we try to do it to the best of our abilities. We will also be willing to learn how to do the job even better. We will try to work in harmony with others because God is also in them. We will strive to be skilled in action so that we can be the best instrument possible.

When the bee comes to suck nectar from a flower, pollen gets stuck to its legs. When it flies to the next flower, it spreads the pollen. By helping plants reproduce, the bee becomes an instrument of Mother Nature. Similarly, when we become an instrument of the Divine, we can enjoy the nectar of divine love and also spread that love to others.

Let us consider what Amma has said on this topic:
- When the flesh of the conch is removed, it can produce a beautiful sound.
- Love and beauty are within you. Try to express them through your actions, and you will definitely touch the very source of bliss.
- Human beings can express love. They can live in love. They can even become love.

Lord Krishna says, "Fix your mind on Me alone and surrender your intellect to Me. There is no doubt that hereafter you will dwell in Me alone." (12.8)

Amma cites the example of how the *gopis* (milkmaids) of Vrindavan labeled their dairy products with the different names of Krishna. They saw Krishna in everyone and everything. Their minds were fixed on Krishna alone.

## A Recounting of Precious Moments with Amma

Sri Ramakrishna Paramahamsa once saw a flock of white seagulls flying against the backdrop of dark rainclouds. The contrasting colors reminded him of his beautiful Mother Kali and he went into *samadhi*. He saw the Divine Mother in everything.

To fix the mind on God all the time is not easy. It requires complete faith in God. We develop faith when we have experiences that reveal God's or the Guru's hand. To discern the hand of the Divine requires awareness. Amma often says that *shraddha*, *bhakti* and *vishvas* — alertness, devotion and faith — form a progression. By developing awareness in every moment of our life, we can experience an awakening of love, which leads to faith.

An incident that took place a few years ago explains this. Melvin, an American devotee in his 80s, visited Amritapuri. While he was here, his lungs became infected and he was sent to AIMS Hospital. An X-ray revealed that he had contracted pneumonia. At that age, pneumonia can be life threatening. His wife immediately called Radhika Nair from the ashram's International Office, and asked her to inform Amma about her husband's critical situation. She did. The next day, the doctors decided to take another X-ray. To their surprise, they found Melvin's lungs completely clear. This miracle boosted Melvin's love for and faith in Amma.

I have experienced something similar. I was in the US then. After graduating from college with a degree in IT, I started looking for a job but could not find one. All the companies wanted someone with job experience. I started doing odd jobs like working in a bookshop; even then I had some karma with books! This went on for about a year. I then left the bookshop job and went to Amritapuri at the end of that year in December. When I went for darshan, Amma told me not to leave my job. I did not understand what she meant, as I had no job. I stayed for two months.

When I returned to the US, I found another temporary job; once again, it was not in the IT field. Every Sunday, I would scan the classifieds for job openings in IT and mail my CV. This went on for about one-and-a-half years. It was then time for Amma's US Tour. When I went for darshan in Chicago, she said, "Don't worry. Amma will take care of things!"

Once again, I could not understand what she was saying. I had a job, money and good health. I had no family problems and was not stressed. Sometimes, it may take us years to understand what the Guru is trying to say. Amma said this on a Saturday. The next day, as usual, I looked for IT job openings in the classifieds. On Monday, I mailed my job applications. On Wednesday, much to my surprise, I received a call for a job interview. I went for the interview on Thursday. The company called back on Friday to offer me a job and asked if I could start work on Monday.

I had been looking for work in the IT field for so long. One week after Amma's darshan, I got this job. I also learned that the manager in the new company was interested in Eastern studies and meditation.

That is when I understood what Amma meant when she said, "Don't worry. Amma will take care of things." Was it just a coincidence? I do not think so. Before this incident, I had a desire to live with Amma in Amritapuri. This event was the clincher. All doubts about going to live with Amma disappeared. I thought that if she could change the flow of my karmic destiny with regards to my work, she could definitely do it for other things such as liberation also. I realized that Amma is a game changer, one who can make the impossible possible.

## A Recounting of Precious Moments with Amma

Lord Krishna says that one in thousands will seek God, and one among those seekers will find him. I firmly believe we all can be that someone because we have Amma with us.

When we have experienced God's protective power,[11] we realize that there is a higher power working behind the scenes to take care of us. We feel safe and secure. Why did Amma help me? I had just met her six months before. She had nothing to gain. Amma did it for the sake of love alone, without wanting anything in return. Through experiences like these, we realize that only God or the Guru loves us unconditionally. This inspires us to dedicate our actions to God or the Guru and become a better instrument in the hands of the Divine.

Lord Krishna says that if we cannot keep our mind on God all the time, we should do spiritual practices to gain concentration of mind. Spiritual practices include Amma's Ma-Om Meditation, White Flower Meditation, IAM™ (Integrated Amrita Meditation), chanting of our mantra, and chanting of the 1,000 names of the Divine Mother. If we cannot do this, Lord Krishna suggests that we dedicate our work to him. If we cannot do even this, then we can surrender the results of our efforts to him. Thus, we come back full circle to karma yoga.

To do karma yoga, we need love. To develop love, we need to engage in karma yoga. They are like two sides of the same coin or the two wings of a bird; its tail is the knowledge of skill in action. May Amma's life of loving and serving others inspire us all to do the same and thus make us a worthy instrument in her hands.

---

[11] Lord Krishna declares, *"na me bhaktah pranashyati"*—"My devotee will never perish" (*Bhagavad Gita*, 9.31)

# 21

## In the Court of Compassion
*Br. Agamamrita Chaitanya*

In the *Bhagavad Gita*, Lord Krishna says:

> *sarva-dharman parityajya mam ekam sharanam vraja*
> *aham tvam sarva-papebhyo mokshayishyami ma shucah*
>
> Give up all kinds of dharma and just surrender to me alone. Do not fear. I shall free you from all sin. (18.66)

The Guru is beyond dharma and adharma and other dualities. Human minds cannot imagine the state of non-duality. The Guru's presence is like a court of compassion. The following verse discusses what our attitude ought to be when approaching the Guru:

> *tad viddhi pranipatena pariprashnena sevaya*
> *upadekshyanti te jnanam jnaninas tattva-darshinah*
>
> To learn the truth, approach a spiritual master. By humbly submitting to the wise, by asking them questions, and by serving them, they, who have realized the Truth, will impart wisdom to you. (4.34)

This verse states three things:
1. what we need to learn;

2. where we can learn it from; and
3. how to learn it.

What we need to learn is the ultimate knowledge, the Truth. What is it? It is described in the previous verse:

> *shreyan dravya-mayad yajnaj jnana-yajnah parantapa*
> *sarvam karmakhilam partha jnane parisamapyate*
>
> O destroyer of enemies, superior to any material sacrifice is the sacrifice of sacred knowledge. O son of Pritha, all work culminates in wisdom. (4.33)

What is the benefit of this knowledge? Lord Krishna says:

> *yajjnatva na punar moham evam yasyasi pandava*
> *yena bhutanyasheshena drakshyasyatmanyatho mayi*
>
> O Arjuna, having gained the highest knowledge, you will never again be deluded. For by this knowledge, you will see that all living beings are in Me, the Supreme. (4.35)

We attain true knowledge when we can see the same self in all beings, both sentient and insentient. Knowing this, everything becomes known.

The next question is where to gain this knowledge. Only a spiritual master, i.e. one who knows the Truth, can impart this knowledge to us. Fortunately for us, the same divine being who dispensed the *Gita* to Arjuna, has incarnated as the Divine Mother, and she is here with us as Amma. Surrendering to the Guru is the only way to escape the miseries of the material world.

What should we do in the presence of the Guru? Lord Krishna gives us clear answers:
- *pranipatena*—by approaching a spiritual master;
- *pariprashnena*—by humble inquiries;
- *sevaya*—by serving.

*Pranipatena:* In order to gain spiritual knowledge, we must have the dedication of a true disciple. In India, prostrating at the Guru's feet is a tradition since time immemorial. The Guru's feet symbolize the path one must tread to attain Self-realization. By prostrating at her feet, we pledge to use body, mind and intellect to attain the ultimate goal. Prostration is also an expression of total surrender. Prostrating to the Guru is not so much a deferring to the Guru's physical body as it is to the principle the Guru represents. Such surrender draws the Guru's grace.

*Pariprashnena:* Asking questions is a time-honored practice of gaining knowledge. Here, the inquiries are those pertaining to spiritual liberation. Asking the Guru such questions keeps the mind focused on spiritual thoughts and makes us more contemplative.

*Sevaya:* Service to the Guru is important. Dedicating actions to the Guru purifies the mind, thus making it befitting for receiving the highest knowledge. When we say the Guru is pleased with the disciple's service, it means that she becomes happy seeing the disciple doing good deeds and thus becoming receptive to divine grace. Serving the Guru does not mean doing chores for the master, but acting with inner purity. Service to the Guru does not have anything to do with physical proximity to her. Remembering

## A Recounting of Precious Moments with Amma

the master in all our actions and doing them selflessly lead to inner purity. As a result, we will be able to assimilate the master's teachings and uplift ourselves spiritually.

To attain this state of mind, we must observe the eight 'limbs' of yoga, namely *yama* (abstinences), *niyama* (observances), *asana* (postures), *pranayama* (breathing), *pratyahara* (withdrawal), *dharana* (concentration), *dhyana* (meditation) and *samadhi* (absorption).

Someone once asked Amma if she could liberate everyone all at once by a mere thought. She said, "It's possible, but who is ready for liberation? Bestowing liberation on one who isn't worthy of it would be like pouring milk into a dirty vessel; the milk will get spoiled."

One must be ready to receive the ultimate knowledge. That is why the scriptures say that the Guru will bestow the highest wisdom only to the disciple who is eligible. Lord Krishna says, *"idam te natapaskaya nabhaktaya kadacana"*—"This knowledge should never ever be given to someone who is not austere or devoted" (*Bhagavad Gita*, 18.67).

In the *Chandogyopanishad*, the story of Shvetaketu shows the importance of being mature enough for spiritual wisdom. His father, Uddalaka, sends Shvetaketu to a *gurukula*. When the son returns home after many years, the father notices that he is puffed up with the ego of scholarship. Uddalaka asks Shvetaketu if he had learned That, knowing which, one would know all. After much debate, Shvetaketu realizes the folly of his pride and ignorance. He surrenders to his Guru and father.

Lord Krishna declares, *"shraddhavan labhate jnanam"*—"One who has *shraddha* (faith) gains divine knowledge" (4.39). Shraddha also refers to the receptivity to divine knowledge, which is self-effulgent. Just as covering a lamp can obscure its light, ignorance hinders true knowledge. Having a thirst for true knowledge can dispel the darkness of ignorance.

The scriptures say that divine knowledge seeks the person with shraddha, and not the other way around:

> *nayamatma pravacanena labhyo na medhaya na bahuna shrutena*
> *yamevaisha vrnute tena labhyastasyaisha atma vivrnute tanum svam*
>
> The Self cannot be attained by studying the Vedas, by intelligence, or by listening. It can be attained only by one who seeks to know it. To such a person, the Self reveals its true nature. (*Kathopanishad*, 1.2.23)

Of course, this does not mean that we need not bother about studying the scriptures, for example, but that our efforts should help us awaken our zeal for knowledge. Nachiketas (from the *Kathopanishad*) had such zeal. He was ready to face even death to attain that wisdom. To such a seeker, everything in nature becomes a Guru.

Amma often explains the same point through the words shraddha, *bhakti* (devotion) and *vishvas* (faith). This reminds me of an incident that took place more than 20 years ago. At that time, the area around the ashram was swampland. We used to do 'sand seva' at night to fill these swamps. On some days, Amma would distribute snacks to us after the seva. One day, Amma made *parippuvada* (lentil fritters) for us. After receiving the prasad, I asked her about shraddha, bhakti and vishvas. Amma said, "Contemplate these topics and find the answer."

Over the years, I discussed the topics with many brahmacharis but none of the answers satisfied me. Let me express my understanding on this matter.

Shraddha is the most important factor in gaining divine knowledge. When Amma uses the word, it denotes awareness in every action. Before operating a machine, we must study its manual. Similarly, in life, we must act only after having gauged and understood the prevailing circumstances. Likewise, as spiritual seekers, we must know why we have come to Amma, what our goal is, how to get there, and why we need to obey the Guru. Real devotion arises only in a mind that acts intelligently. In the beginning, our devotion might be based on fear of God—*bhaya bhakti*. Later, it evolves into *prema bhakti*, loving devotion, which helps us develop unshakeable faith, which, in turn, helps us attain true knowledge.

Amma always reminds us, "Don't think that Amma is confined to her physical body. There is an Amma within each one of you who assesses all your actions and thoughts. The outer Amma might forgive everything but the inner Amma will judge every action."

The main obstacle to attaining divine knowledge is the ego, which is insidious by nature. The following fable explains this. There was a yogi who used to do penance in a cave for three months at a time without even drinking water. After those three months, he would emerge from the cave. People from the surrounding villages would be waiting to see him. They would offer him fruits and seek his blessings. After that, the yogi would return to the cave and remain there for the next three months, steeped in penance.

Many years passed. One day, a *mahatma* (spiritually illumined soul) visited the village. The villagers went to get his blessings. All of them told the mahatma about the yogi. At first, the mahatma did not say anything. But when people continued to sing the yogi's praises, he said, "You don't understand. This yogi eats every day!"

The villagers thought that the mahatma was jealous of the yogi and did not believe him. To prove the truth of his assertion, the mahatma suggested a plan. The villagers agreed. After two days, the yogi came out of his cave after three months of penance. To his shock, there wasn't even a single villager waiting for him outside. Two days later, the villagers accompanied the mahatma to see the yogi. They found him dead. The mahatma said, "He had been feeding on the praise you lavished on him." This fable illustrates the subtle nature of the ego.

The scriptures come alive in the divine presence of a true master. The Guru's presence is like a powerful beam revealing the dormant ego within the disciple. Only when this ego dies can the intellect lead us to true knowledge. Amma orchestrates circumstances to show us our ego. She once said, "Children, Amma has scattered many valuable gemstones and pearls. You can pick up as many of them as you want. Do not squander this precious opportunity." What exactly are these gems? They are the varied circumstances in which she reveals how the ego rears its head.

How blessed we all are! With how much care and love Amma is leading us all to the goal! I recall an incident that Br. Bodhamrita narrated to me. It took place near the Bhavani River during one of Amma's Tamil Nadu Tours. While everyone went to swim in the river, Amma asked Bodhamritaji to follow her to another bank. Amma then asked him to tie one end of a cloth

## A Recounting of Precious Moments with Amma

around his neck and to hold the other end out. She dived into a deep part of the river, collected some clams, and put them into the outstretched cloth. She did this three times. Then, placing her palm on the clams, she said, "Will you all live righteously at least in the next birth by serving others?" She remained silent for a while and then walked back. To think that Amma takes pains to spiritually elevate even clams at a remote location. How blessed we are to have such a compassionate master.

May we all be able to recognize her immeasurable compassion and try to eradicate our ego. By doing so, we can become a conch issuing the Lord's clarion calls or a flute producing the lambent music of the soul.

# 22

## Self-effort and Divine Grace
*Br. Sravanamrita Chaitanya*

Amma says that to achieve anything, we need to put in self-effort, but for self-effort to bear fruit, divine grace is necessary. Consider the following verse from the *Bhagavad Gita*:

> *tasmat tvam uttishtha yasho labhasva*
> *jitva shatrun bhunkshva rajyam samrddham*
> *mayaivaite nihatah purvam eva*
> *nimitta-matram bhava savya-sacin*

> Therefore, arise and acquire glory. Conquer your enemies and enjoy a prosperous kingdom. They have already been killed by me. O Arjuna, just be an instrument. (11.33)

This verse highlights the four factors behind success: motivation, self-effort, remembrance of the goal, and divine grace.

There is a maxim in Sanskrit that underscores the necessity of effort:

> *udayamenaiva hi sidhyanti karyani na manorathaih*
> *na hi suptasya simhasya pravishanti mukhe mrigah*

> Work gets done by effort and not merely by wishing. Deer do not enter the mouth of a sleeping lion.

## A Recounting of Precious Moments with Amma

Swami Vivekananda often highlighted the importance of self-effort. It seems that he once told a young and lazy man to go and do some work, any work; even stealing something was better than his present state of idleness, he said. Not that Swami Vivekananda was advocating thievery. He was making the point that engaging in action is better than sitting idle.

Amma gives an example to illustrate the importance of self-effort. During her childhood, her mother, Damayanti-amma, used to rear hens. Often, after laying eggs, they would get so used to brooding on them that they would not even get up to move around. Knowing that this inertia could lead to their death, Damayanti-amma would throw them into the backwaters in order to force them to start flapping their wings and move. This would revitalize the hens, which would once again walk and eat.

In the *Ramayana*, when it was time to cross the ocean, Hanuman feels defeated even before he has made the attempt. He is unaware of his own power. At that moment, Jambavan motivates Hanuman and rouses his dormant powers. Stirred by Jambavan's words, Hanuman takes a mighty leap across the ocean and reaches Lanka.

In the *Mahabharata*, the valiant Pandava prince, Arjuna, decides to take up arms to defend the righteous cause of the Pandavas. But after coming to the battlefield and seeing his relatives arrayed against him, he gets cold feet. He wants to throw in the towel and renounce the world. His desire to quit the war and the world is motivated not by right knowledge but a debilitating attachment to his near and dear ones. This was contrary to dharma, which is doing the right thing at the right time at the right place in the right way with the right attitude.

In a bid to galvanize him into action, Lord Krishna criticizes Arjuna:

*kutastva kashmalamidam vishame samupasthitam
anarya-jushtam-asvargyam-akirtikaram-arjuna*

Arjuna, how has this delusion gripped you at this critical time? It is dishonorable and disgraceful, and will lead you away from heaven. (2.2)

*klaibyam ma sma gamah partha naitattvayyupapadyate
kshudram hridaya-daurbalyam tyaktvottishtha parantapa*

Yielding to such faint-heartedness does not befit you, Arjuna. Cast off this demeaning weakness and arise, O conqueror of enemies! (2.3)

Actually, Arjuna was a warrior par excellence. He had defeated the Kaurava army single-handedly while in exile. He was the master of many skills besides archery, and possessed many rare and divine weapons. Further, he had so much control over his mind that he came to be known as *Jitakama*, one who has conquered desire, after he proved himself able to withstand the temptations of even celestial nymphs. Arjuna was also called *Gudakesha*, one who has gained control over sleep. But in this situation, overpowered by his emotions and attachments, he proved unequal to his dharma.

Certain situations bring out our negativities. Amma often illustrates this with the story of the snake frozen by snow. It was lying motionless in the deep cold of a Himalayan pass. A passerby chanced on the snake, which seemed tame and harmless, picked it up, and held it close to his chest. His body heat thawed the frozen snake, which started to move. Its innate nature manifested itself

## A Recounting of Precious Moments with Amma

and it bit the man, who died on the spot. Similarly, our *vasanas* (latent tendencies) will manifest in conducive circumstances.

Amma tells us such stories so that we can better appreciate the import of scriptural teachings. Often, to understand the concepts expounded in the scriptures, we need to engage in protracted study and contemplation. However, in the presence of a Guru, we can understand and assimilate sublime spiritual principles much faster, as she feeds us with the nectar of knowledge. The Guru is truly marvelous.

Once, someone asked Amma, "How do you know about family life or solutions to marital problems when you have never been married?"

Amma's reply was spontaneous: "The driver of a vehicle need not know everything about it, whereas its manufacturer will."

Another person asked her, "Amma, you have millions of devotees all over the world. How do you know when something happens to one of them?"

This was her response: "How many strands of hair do you have on your body? Won't you feel the pain if even one strand is plucked? All my children are a part of me."

Amma's answers reveal her omniscience and the reassurance that she is with us all the time. However, this does not mean that we can abstain from self-effort. Our duty is to act with the humbling awareness that it is God's power that enables to do anything. The following verse makes the same point:

> *na tatra suryo bhati na candratarakam*
> *nema vidyuto bhanti kutoyamagnih*
> *tameva bhantamanubhati sarvam*
> *tasya bhasa sarvamidam vibhati*

> The sun shines not; nor do the moon, lightning or fire. All these shine by the light of Brahman alone.
> (*Kathopanishad*, 2.2.15)

Amma tells a story that drives homes the importance of acting as an instrument in God's hands. Once, in a village square, there was a statue of a *mahatma* (spiritually illumined soul) who had done many good deeds for the villagers during his time. As a tribute to his humanitarian work, the statue was built with outstretched arms. The plaque under the statue was inscribed with the words, 'Come into my arms.'

Over the years, the arms of the statue yielded to wear and tear, and fell off. Seeing this, the villagers became upset. They gathered together to decide what to do. Some suggested that a new statue be built. Others felt that new arms should be made. After much wrangling, an old man got up and said, "Let's leave the statue the way it is." Hearing this, one man reminded him about the inscription on the plaque: 'Come into my arms.' The old man replied, "No problem. Just add the words 'by letting me work through yours' below the existing inscription."

Similarly, Amma says that we should become the hands, eyes and ears of God, i.e. become an instrument in his hands. In this way, we can draw ever closer to the Divine. Just as Arjuna drew inspiration from Lord Krishna, we can draw inspiration, strength and courage from Amma.

However, more often than not, we forget that the power to act is not ours, and we arrogantly take credit for our successes. A story from the *Kenopanishad* illustrates this.

Once, after winning a war with the *asuras* (demons), the *devas* (gods) became arrogant, thinking that they had won the battle owing to their own superior might. To make them realize the folly of their thinking, a *yaksha* (celestial being) appeared before them. The devas sent Agni, the god of fire, to investigate the identity of the yaksha. Agni went to the yaksha and said, "I can burn anything!" The yaksha placed a blade of grass before Agni and challenged him to burn it. Agni could not do so, though he tried hard. Defeated, he returned to the other devas, who sent Vayu, the god of wind. Vayu could not nudge the blade of grass by even an inch. Next, the devas sent Indra, the lord of the devas, to the yaksha, who disappeared. In its place, there appeared Goddess Uma, a form of *shakti* (divine power). She told him that the yaksha was none other than Brahman, the Supreme, and that it was by His power that devas had attain victory in battle.

In truth, nothing in this world happens because of us; it happens only because of God's grace. As Amma often says, we need divine grace even to close our mouth after we yawn.

That is what Lord Krishna meant when he said '*nimitta-matram bhava savya-sacin*'—' O exemplary archer, perform your action as an instrument in my hands.' In saying so, the Lord is giving Arjuna the guarantee of success, for Arjuna is merely an instrument; the Lord has already determined the outcome.

In the final verse of the *Bhagavad Gita*, we see the Lord in the form of grace and Arjuna representing self-effort.

> *yatra yogeshvarah krishno yatra partho dhanur-dharah*
> *tatra shrir-vijayo bhutir-dhruva nitir-matir-mama*

> Where there is Lord Krishna, the Master of all yoga, and where there is Arjuna, the expert archer, there will undoubtedly be prosperity, victory and righteousness!
> (18.78)

Just as the sun does not need the light from a candle, Amma requires nothing from us. We are very fortunate that we have Amma in our life, inspiring us by her own example. May we become open enough to let her work through us. In this way, we can serve the world as a tool in her divine hands.

# 23

## Mother Nature
*Br. Sarvagatamrita Chaitanya*

For some years now, Amma has been reminding us that both nature and human minds are in an agitated state. In hindsight, her words strike us as prescient. Great masters are like that. They give us only hints of what is going to happen. If they openly reveal impending disasters, they know that most of us will live in fear. Spiritual masters are also not interested in being seen as soothsayers. Their only interest is in helping us become prepared for such eventualities.

If we study the universe, we will see that it has an innate rhythm and harmony. However, when our lives deviate from spiritual values and when we live according to our likes and dislikes, this subtle balance is adversely affected. Among the life forms on earth, only human beings have been endowed with the power of discernment. In spite of that, we have exploited natural resources ruthlessly, causing natural disasters.

The history of humankind is a chronicle of our attempts to conquer nature. The rampant use of chemical fertilizers and pesticides has poisoned our food, air and water. Mobile towers and the radiation from them have endangered the lives of small birds and bees. According to some reports, there has been a 50% reduction in the bird population in recent years. Frogs are being captured and exported, leading to a proliferation of small insects that damage crops. In short, the harmony between human beings and nature has been lost.

Earlier, when farmers sowed sesame seeds, they would coat the seeds with rice powder and sow rice grains along with the seeds so that the ants would take the rice and leave the seeds. That was how thoughtful our ancestors were; they considered the welfare even of ants while cultivating crops. They worshipped Mother Nature as a visible form of the Divine, and so treated her with respect and reverence.

The recent spate of natural disasters suggest that we have crossed certain limits. What can we do to redress this imbalance?

In the third chapter of the *Bhagavad Gita*, Lord Krishna speaks about *yajna bhava*—the attitude of performing each action as an offering to God. Amma often reminds us that each and every being in creation has a role to play, just as every screw in an engine is vital. Understanding this paves the way to finding solutions to the problems we are facing today.

Lord Krishna says, *"parasparam bhavayantah shreyah param avapsyatha"*—"By mutual cooperation, you shall gain prosperity" (*Bhagavad Gita*, 3.11).

There is divine consciousness in all things, both sentient and insentient, and the more we invoke that divinity, the more we are likely to succeed. Suppose we are trying to bring a mango down from a tree by throwing a stone at it. Several factors must come together before we can succeed: we must be able to lift our hand; we must be able to hurl the stone hard enough and accurately; the winds should not be unfavorable…

The scriptures mention the *pancamahayajna* (five great sacrifices) that everyone is expected to perform:

## 1. Deva Yajna
This refers to ritual fire sacrifices in which oblations are offered to the gods. Our ancestors believed that the gods must be propitiated so that we do not suffer much. The fire sacrifices performed as part of Deva Yajna have a salubrious effect on the environment.

## 2. Brahma Yajna
This sacrifice involves teaching and/or studying the scriptures. This form of worship honors Brahman, the Supreme. We ought to revere the scriptures and our Guru, for they alone enable our spiritual growth. The two pillars of this yajna are *satya* (truth) and *dharma* (righteousness). In India, there have always been people who spurned wealth and riches to embark on the path to the ultimate truth. The best gift we can give the Guru, as an expression of our gratitude, is following the path she has shown us.

## 3. Pitr Yajna
This sacrifice refers to the offering of food and water to one's ancestors. Amma often reminds us that the best way to honor them is to respect, love and take care of them while they are living. For this reason, treating our parents and grandparents well is also a part of pitr yajna.

These days, one hears of more cases of children neglecting their parents or washing their hands of them by consigning them to care homes. While celebrating Father's Day and Mother's Day is laudable, we must not forget to express our gratitude to them daily.

Once, a man and his elderly father were quarreling. In the heat of the moment, the son pushed the father out of his house. As he stood outside the door, the old man started laughing. Seeing this, the son became furious and dragged his father out of the gate and locked it. The father continued laughing. The neighbor, who was watching all this, asked the elderly man, "Why are you laughing? How can you remain calm when your own son is behaving like this?"

The old man replied, "When I was young, I pushed my father only out of the door. But my son pushed me out of the gate. Thinking about what my grandson is going to do to my son, I cannot stop laughing!"

The best way in which parents can impart the value of filial piety to their children is by practicing it themselves. Children learn from and follow their parents. Amma says that if we keep treading on grass, a path will be formed in time. In the same way, whatever is taught to children while they are young will create an indelible impression on their minds. In Amrita Vidyalayam,[12] students are taught to perform *pada puja* (ceremonial washing of the feet) to their parents.

In the olden days, grandma stories were often the first source of values for children. Now, with parents working and extended families becoming more uncommon, the transmission of values is becoming weak. This has a far-reaching effect on society.

### 4. Nru Yajna

This refers to the sacrifices to be made for people. Amma says that any help that we render must be given with due caution and discernment. Also, we ought to help without expectation of reward. Most people offer with the expectation that the person they helped will return the favor sooner than later. This attitude is

---

[12] National network of schools managed by the Mata Amritanandamayi Math offering value-based education.

wrong, says Amma. It reflects the sentiment commonly expressed as "I love you." Amma says that the very words imply duality, a separation between 'I' and 'you.' In such a relationship, love is conditional and predicated on reciprocation. The ideal sentiment is "I am love." In this sentence, unconditional love is one's very nature.

**5. Bhuta Yajna**
This sacrifice refers to the offering of food and drinks to birds and beasts. In Sanatana Dharma,[13] all beings are considered divine and worshipped as such. That is why there are temples for snakes, spiders, lizards and monkeys in India. There is a special food offering ceremony for animals in many temples. Crows are considered embodiments of ancestral spirits and they are given a part of the food cooked daily at home.

Each deity in the Hindu pantheon is also associated with an animal that serves as his or her vehicle. All these actions and ideas originate from the understanding that the same divine power dwells in all other beings in creation.

This entire universe can be considered a single body with innumerable cells. If there is a disruption in the inner workings, the system will begin a cleansing process to set things right. The human race is now the most dangerous virus threatening nature. We think that everything in nature is for our taking and have been thoughtlessly plundering the resources of earth for our selfish needs. We have recklessly hunted animals, polluted the air, water and soil, and flattened hills and mountains.

---

[13] Literally, 'Eternal Religion,' the original and traditional name of Hinduism.

The coronavirus pandemic has thrown a spanner in our selfish works and humbled the whole world. People are not able to leave the confines of their home. Could it be that COVID-19 is an antibody for our septic behavior? What is the solution to the problems facing humankind?

Heeding Amma's counsel. Through her every word and deed, she continues to proclaim the timeless wisdom of the ancient *rishis* (seers). We must cultivate the same reverential attitude of our ancestors, who saw creation as the manifest form of the Creator.

In Sanskrit, the word for tree is *'taru,'* which also means that which protects. Owing to widespread deforestation, nature's green lungs are being destroyed, thus ruining the health of planet earth. Our ancestors conveyed the value of a single tree through the following saying:

> *dasha-kupa-sama vapi dasha-vapi-samo hrdah*
> *dasha-hrada-samah putro dasha-putra samo drumah*

> A pond is equal to ten wells. A reservoir is worth ten such ponds. Ten such reservoirs are the same as a (noble) son. A tree is equal to ten such sons. (*Padma Purana*, 1.43.442)

We must learn from the book of nature. Each object in nature is a page in that book. Human beings are just one among the myriad of pages in the book of nature. The *Ishavasya Upanishad* declares, *"isha vasyamidam sarvam"*—"Everything in the universe is pervaded by God" (1). We must regard and revere all of nature as we would our own mother.

In India, it is believed that we have five mothers, namely:

## A Recounting of Precious Moments with Amma

1. *Deha Mata* (biological mother): she is the one who gave birth to us and brought us up with great love and sacrifice. Her love is the closest earthly approximation to divine love. The mother is also the first Guru.
2. *Bhu Mata* (earth): she provides us with everything, including food, clothing and shelter. Amma says that our birth mother may let us sit in her lap for a few years, whereas Mother Earth keeps us in her lap our whole life. Instead of appreciating how she continues to nourish us, we are exploiting and harming her.
3. *Go Mata* (cow): Amma often cites the cow as an exemplar of taking the minimum and giving the maximum. In return for just some grass and water, it generously gives us nourishing milk. Even cow dung and urine have beneficial properties. Cow dung is used as manure and cow urine is used as an ingredient in medicine. Amma has spoken about people who used to earn a living from rearing just one or two cows at home.
4. *Veda Mata* (the Vedas): the repository of all the knowledge that the rishis perceived. The Vedas are a manifest form of God.
5. *Ganga Mata* (the Ganges): the water from this holy river is said to purify body and mind and absolve one who takes a dip in it, of all sin.

The universe is the totality of all these elements. Amma's green initiatives are not just an environmental project but a graceful gesture from the Mother of the Universe to help us awaken love and reverence for nature. These green initiatives, which highlight the need to restore the lost harmony in nature, include kitchen gardens; *Vishu-tai-neettam*, an annual sapling planting drive in association with Vishu, traditionally considered the New Year in Kerala; the sacred groves project, aimed at restoring the tradition of sacred groves; Amala Bharatam, a nation-wide cleanup campaign; Haritateeram, the planting of trees along the seacoast; making beehives; starting organic gardens; recycling...

When the Amala Bharatam campaign was launched in 2010, Amma appealed to people to stop spitting in public places, saying that it was unhygienic. With the coronavirus pandemic ravaging the world, Amma's advice seems all the more noteworthy.

From around 2017, Amma started guiding her children all over the world in the White Flowers Meditation. By collectively praying for and visualizing the healing of the planet, Amma believes that we make a difference to the environment; such is the power of this meditation. Further, praying for the welfare of others purifies our mind and makes our hearts more expansive. Amma gives the example of how much satisfaction we will feel when we feed a hungry orphan. Similarly, when we pray for the world, the fruits of those prayers will reach us as well.

Amma is the rarest of spiritual masters who has turned her birthplace into an ashram. How can we ever repay the care and compassion she has shown us? Amma does not need or expect anything from us. However, we can avail of the opportunities to grow spiritually if we follow the path of truth and dharma and do our *sadhana* (spiritual practices) with zeal and sincerity.

Many of us have been blessed with the opportunity to meet Amma and have her darshan. Perhaps, this was the fruit of meritorious deeds we did in the past. Amma says that we are all beads strung together on the same thread of love. She is trying to awaken that unconditional love and compassion within us all.

As Amma's children, we have nothing to fear. All we need to do is obey her.

May Amma remain here on earth for many long years so that she can continue to spread her light and love in this world. O Amma, your children have no refuge other than you. I offer this prayer at Amma's holy feet.

# 24

## Leading the World with Love
*Br. Mokshamrita Chaitanya*

Everyone faces challenges in life. The question is how well we can handle them. If we cannot do so effectively, then the situation will overpower us. But if we can, then we will become a leader. Every challenge or problem is an opportunity to manifest our leadership potential. For some, that seed of leadership becomes a tree, whereas in others, that seed does not even sprout.

In my opinion, the most important criterion for becoming a world leader is knowing what love is; not the love between individuals but love for all beings in this world; Love with a capital L. There is only one such person who comes to my mind: Amma. Her religion is Love.

Life around Amma is full of joy and positive energy. Those who live with Amma are some of the happiest people on earth. When we are with Amma, care and concern for others automatically develop in our hearts. We learn to do *seva* (selfless service) out of love and not obligation. Amma creates an atmosphere of celebration around her, no matter where she is. Even if there is chaos around her, she is not affected. Around Amma, we learn to accept life as it is and still celebrate it.

Amma's life reminds one of Lord Krishna in the battlefield of *Mahabharata*. Though there was chaos all around him, Krishna faced everything with a smile. After meeting Amma for the first time, I felt strongly that if there was anyone who could teach me how to live life deeply and fully, it was Amma. I am glad I took that decision to be with Amma. It was the best decision of my life. Every day with Amma since then has been a celebration.

Amma's background is humble. Her father was a fisherman. She received only primary education. Yet her spiritual wisdom, humanitarian efforts and philanthropic outreach are unparalleled. The United Nations awarded Amma the Gandhi King Award for Peace and Non violence. Universities have bestowed honorary PhD's on her. She has been invited to deliver keynote addresses at international fora such as the Interfaith Alliance for Safer Communities (Abu Dhabi, 2018), UN Academic Impact Conference on Technology for Sustainable Development (New York, 2015), and the Joint Declaration of Religious Leaders Against Modern Slavery (Vatican, 2014).

**Humanitarian Work**

Her service activities are wide ranging. Amma has made significant contributions in the domain of empowering women. In addition, her untiring efforts to provide free healthcare, food, clothing, houses, pension schemes for the old, scholarships and vocational training demonstrate her commitment to uplifting the downtrodden.

Amma is also inspiring youth all over the world to support environmental projects such as the UN Billion Tree Campaign. AYUDH, the youth wing of the M.A. Math, is empowering young people to become compassionate leaders with a sense of tolerance, solidarity and global responsibility.

Be it a ₹200-*crore* (2 billion) relief-and-rehabilitation aid package following the 2004 tsunami, a million-dollar relief package in aid of Hurricane Katrina victims, a ₹100-crore (1 billion) relief-and-rehabilitation scheme following the flash floods that struck Uttarakhand, or the five-crore-rupee (50 million) relief package for the survivors of the 2019 Pulwama attack, Amma has been at the forefront of reaching out to and helping those most in need. To quote Nobel Peace Prize winner Prof. Muhammad Yunus, "Amma has done more work than many governments have ever done for their people. Her contribution is enormous."

## Compassionate Leadership

Management books speak of different styles of leadership:
- democratic leadership, in which members of the group play a participative role in decision making;
- autocratic leadership, in which one person makes decisions largely without consulting others;
- laissez-faire leadership, in which leadership roles are delegated to subordinates;
- strategic leadership, in which the leader is able to influence members of the team to accept his or her vision for the organization and to act accordingly;
- transformational leadership, in which the leader encourages, inspires and motivates employees to innovate and create change; and
- transactional leadership, in which the focus is on supervision, organization and performance of employees.

With Amma, however, I have experienced a totally different kind of leadership: compassionate leadership. In this style of leadership, compassion is the basis of all interactions. It is about putting oneself in the shoes of others and about being able to motivate and touch the lives of others in a way that empowers them and makes them self-reliant.

Amma's darshan is a spontaneous expression of the love she feels towards the whole of creation. Swami Amritageetananda once defined Amma's signature hug as 'Human Union with God,' both the inner and outer God. Through her warm embrace, Amma invokes the divinity within us.

In his book *'Color of the Rainbow,'* Swami Amrita-swarupananda (Swamiji) describes Amma as a CEO, Chief Enlightened Overseer. Amma is a compassionate overseer, whose presence motivates everyone to perform. Compassion is second nature to Amma, and that is why she draws all kinds of people to her. The Amritapuri Ashram is a mini-world. People from all nations and of all faiths live harmoniously under one roof. Someone once asked Swamiji why the title of his book does not refer to the 'colors' (as opposed to 'color') of the rainbow. He replied, "Just as a rainbow represents both unity and diversity, Amma is the supreme consciousness pervading this world of diversity."

Unless leaders establish a deep connection with others, they cannot lead them. Amma says that managing 100 employees means managing 100 minds, and unless one can manage one's own mind first, one cannot manage the minds of others. Amma's leadership is even more radical because she works at the level of the heart. In an interview published in the June 2017 issue of 'The Week,' Amma said:

> Love and compassion are the two fundamental principles of life… Out of ignorance and ego, we keep abandoning these two principles. People belonging to various belief systems are determined to force their views on others. This naturally leads to a lack of understanding

and culminates in conflict and war. We should ask ourselves, 'Why do we want to enforce our perspective on another person? Why can't we let others live peacefully with their own way of thinking and faith?'... There is war and misery everywhere in the world. It is impossible to change that in one stroke. But individuals can be transformed through love and compassion.
I have tremendous faith in that because I see that transformation happening around me every day—a very tangible change.

**Spiritual Wisdom**

Religion is only a stepping stone to spirituality. Even though religions are many, they must all converge finally in the spirit of oneness and kinship. That is true spirituality. Amma sees unity in diversity. She is established in that highest principle of non-duality. Her life is her message.

Amma does not waste even a single minute. She utilizes time and resources effectively for the betterment of society and the world at large. Her darshan sessions typically last for more than 12 hours, and she does not take any break for rest or refreshments. If asked whether she does not get tired of doing this day in and day out, Amma smiles and says, "If your actions are done with love, you won't feel tired or bored. I am like a river and my nature is to flow."

Her days are packed back-to-back, especially when she travels by road across the length and breadth of India, North America, and Europe. She could fly but chooses to save every single penny to help the poor and needy; she also wants to set an example of simple living. Though she has been traveling all over the world

## A Recounting of Precious Moments with Amma

since 1987, Amma has never gone sightseeing or taken a vacation even once. Wherever she is, her sole priority is receiving people, dispelling their sorrows, sharing her love and wisdom, and motivating them. She says, "To lovingly caress people, to console and wipe away their tears until the end of this mortal frame; this is Amma's wish."

After Ms. Yolanda King, Daughter of Rev. Dr. Martin Luther King Jr., met Amma, she said, "I had the blessed privilege and honor to meet Amma and receive darshan during her U.S. Tour. It was a moment of transcendence, for I was able to grasp for the first time the essence of true fulfillment and agape love. What I cherish about Amma is that she not only talks the talk and is the embodiment of unconditional love, but she expresses that love in action. She walks the talk. Mahatma Gandhi urged us to 'be the change we wish to see in the world.' Amma is the change she wants to see in our world. She is a profound living example for all of us."

It is a misconception that a leader is someone who tells people what to do and what not to do. A true leader is always ready to listen. Amma accepts us as we are. She comes down to our level of understanding and uplifts us. She does not try to suppress our nature but helps us channel our energies for our own good and that of society.

Once, a young man told Amma that he was feeling sad because his girlfriend had broken up with him. Amma made him sit near her, spoke to him, and consoled him. Amma then said that she would give him a new girlfriend. The boy was surprised. Amma said, "This new girlfriend will never leave you and you can speak to her anytime you want. Dear son, this new girlfriend is called Nature. If you love nature, she will never leave you or cheat you.

You can talk to plants and rivers, and slowly, you will find that they, too, talk back to you."

This proved to be a turning point in his life. He took Amma's words seriously and became a true nature lover.

Amma listens to the problems of people, consoles them and offers solutions. This is not an easy task. A study conducted at Antioch University of Seattle revealed that 81% of psychologists develop mental problems later in their life. They are prone to experiencing burnout and compassion fatigue. If not managed well, the high levels of distress can impair job efficiency. Amma has been listening to the problems of people for decades, but nothing has affected her functionality. Everywhere she goes, Amma leaves behind the mesmerizing fragrance of love that transforms people.

**Inspiration**

Dr. P. Venkat Rangan is a computer scientist and current Vice-Chancellor of Amrita University. He received the President of India's gold medal from the Indian Institute of Technology Madras in 1984. A pioneering researcher in multimedia systems, he was the founder and director of the Multimedia Laboratory at the University of California, San Diego. Dr. Rangan also founded Yodlee Inc. and served as its CEO, for which he was selected in 2000 as one of the 25 best entrepreneurs by the President of the USA and was featured on the July 2000 cover of Internet World Magazine. He left his lucrative career in the US to join Amma's mission.

Dr. Shanti Nair, Director, Nanosciences, Center for Nanosciences, Kochi, received the Presidential Young Investigator Award from President Ronald Reagan for research in composite materials. In February 2009, he received the MRSI (Materials Research Society of India) Medal for outstanding contributions in the field of Materials Science. He received the Prestigious National Research Award from the Government of India in 2011 for research in Nanosciences. In 2014, Dr. Nair received the CNR Rao India Nanosciences Award for outstanding contributions in Nanotechnology Research and Development in India. He, too, is now part of Amma's mission. Dr. Nair declares, "Amma is the inspiration behind all my research."

These two names highlight the reverse brain drain trend that Amma inspired. Many other people have also returned to India because of Amma. Why did they abandon luxury and comfort for life in a one-room apartment in a remote coastal village in India? Clearly, they found something higher and more valuable in Amma's presence.

According to Maslow's Hierarchy of Needs, there are five kinds of needs: psychological, safety, belongingness and love, esteem and self-actualization. The Hindu scriptures speak about the four *purusharthas* (objects of human pursuit): *moksha* (spiritual liberation), *dharma* (righteousness), *artha* (prosperity) and *kama* (pleasure). Those who serve Amma find their needs (from Maslow's Hierarchy) met. In addition, they find that they are on the path to spiritual liberation, the highest potential of life.

Marc Russell Benioff is the founder, chairman and CEO of Salesforce, an enterprise cloud computing company, and a renowned philanthropist. When he was about 30 years old, Benioff recounts his first meeting with Amma when he visited Amritapuri with his friend Arjun. He said, "Arjun and I were sitting in a little hut with a Guru... Arjun was getting ready to start this new venture capital company... he took out his business plan and he started reading it to the saint. And for an hour he talked about the future of technology... And she sat there so patiently, for an hour... After listening to his whole business plan, she turned to him and said, 'Arjun, while you are working so hard to change the world and create all this great technology, and I'm sure all of it will come to pass, don't forget, don't forget to do something for others.'... I felt like she was talking to me. And I kind of felt like I'd just found what I was looking for."

After meeting Amma, actor Jim Carrey said, "I was feeling down about life and love. Then I met a woman named Ammachi, and she gave me back my smile. Darkness cannot compete with her." Indian actress Vidya Balan said, "Amma shows us that we are worthy of acceptance, we are worthy of love. That message for me is beyond religion, beyond politics. Amma is the embodiment of pure love."

Amma is the Chancellor of Amrita University. She meets researchers from the university once a week, discusses their work with them, gives them guidance, and, like a mother, distributes snacks to them. Has there ever been such an accessible and loving chancellor?

In 2019, during Amma's program in Munich, Margarete Bause, Member of Parliament, said, "Amma's work is so infinitely valuable, especially at a time so often marked by hatred and violence, by poverty and exploitation, by division and exclusion. Amma, with your work, you give hope. You are a role model for many people. It would be desirable for decision-makers in politics and business to take you as their role model. For me, as a human rights politician, you stand for exactly what the first article of the Universal Declaration of Human Rights says: 'All human beings are born free and equal in dignity and rights.'"

# A Recounting of Precious Moments with Amma

When Alice Walker, who won the Pulitzer Prize for Fiction and the National Book Award for Fiction in 1983 for her novel *The Color Purple*, met Amma, she remarked, "Amma presents the kind of leadership we need for our planet to survive. This is the most heroic person I've probably ever met."

## Wonder

Only human beings can feel wonder and awe. Only we can be stirred by a sunset, marvel at the stars, and glory in our achievements. Amma is a living and walking wonder. After meeting Amma, Dr. Lee Hartwell, a Nobel Laureate said, "The experience of her personality is unique and very moving. I do not feel any desire to reduce it to something I can understand intellectually. It is a sense of mystery."

Amma guides projects in fields as diverse as wireless sensors, biotechnology, nanotechnology, cybersecurity and e-learning. Her ability to switch effortlessly from one field to another is remarkable. She could be talking to the head of one of her institutions one moment. In the very next moment, Amma can talk to a child, coming down to his or her level. This ability to multi-task with such perfection is rare. Dr. Vijay Bhatkar, known as the father of India's supercomputing, once said, "Amma is faster than a supercomputer."

In spite of her stupendous abilities, Amma is simple and humble. Her simplicity, humility and compassion touch our hearts deeply because of her irrefutable motherliness. Amma says, "The need of the hour is motherhood." Motherhood is not about giving birth but enveloping the world with love. It is said that behind every successful man is a woman. I would like to change that saying a little: "Behind every successful person is a mother."

Amma is not interested in being hailed as a world leader. In fact, she wants to be a servant of the world. She has also often said, "What the world needs today are not leaders but servants." There cannot be a better definition than that describing what a leader ought to be like. A leader is ever ready to serve others. One who wants others to serve him/her can never be a good leader.

**Conclusion**
Before meeting Amma, I had a deep desire to live with a Self-realized master, a Guru, but never in my wildest dreams did I think that I would live in a seaside ashram in a remote village of Kerala. However, Amma's love was so irresistible that I was drawn like an iron filing to a powerful magnet.

After joining the ashram, I thought I would never touch computers again. I had dreams about meditating and studying the scriptures all day long. But Amma guides us in a way that makes any task a meditation and every experience a book of learning. Under Amma's guidance, I began teaching engineering students, authored several research papers, started singing and composing, and even delivered a TEDx talk. Looking back, I see that all this was possible because of the confidence Amma instilled in me. Her love and grace are my only qualifications.

Sometimes I wish that everyone in the world would get Amma's hug at least once in their life. For if everyone can experience true and selfless love at least once, I am sure each person will be transformed sooner or later into someone who truly loves and cares for others. Today, what we need the most is this love, which alone can make us truly humane. I have hope for the world because Amma is with us. If only we could all see who she really is and walk in her footsteps, the world will become a heaven.

Amma says, "Let us all light the lamp of hope, compassion and unity. If each one of us lights a small lamp, the strength of that light will multiply and everything can be illumined. May our selfless actions combined with divine grace protect the world."

# 25

# World Leader
*Bri. Visvapriyamrita Chaitanya*

The word 'leadership' conjures different ideas for different people. Perhaps because the *seva* (service activity) Amma entrusted me is in the field of education, whenever I hear the word leadership, the image that comes to my mind is that of a school election. In Amma's Amrita Vidyalayam schools, teachers do not choose student leaders. Students choose their leaders. It has often surprised me to see how they do so.

Often, the student who gets elected is not one with a stellar academic performance, good looks, wealth or popularity. He or she is likely to be someone who once helped a wounded child receive first-aid, who took the initiative to find a classmate's lost pen or notebook, or who represented the class in taking up a matter with the principal. In short, children who exhibit qualities like courage, selflessness and service mindedness are the ones most likely to be chosen as leaders.

There is a leader even in a forest—the lion, who is considered king of the forest. It doesn't wear a crown, collect taxes from other animals, or stand in any election, and yet, it is the undisputed king of the beasts. How and why? By virtue of its grandeur, awareness of its own strength, and the principles it lives by.

If we look at the Puranas, we will see that Lord Krishna is extolled as an exemplary leader. Right from his childhood, he exhibited all the qualities of a leader. He was always the ringleader of the *gopas* (cowherd boys), whether in grazing the cows, at play, or in times of danger. Krishna stole butter but did so only to satiate the hunger of his friends and to captivate the hearts of the *gopis* (milkmaids), and not for any selfish reason. Thus, everyone in the village looked up to the darling child of Vrindavan.

Amma's story is similar. During her school days, seeing some classmates trying to stave off their hunger by drinking water, she understood that their parents could not afford to provide them lunch. Amma started sharing her lunch with them. Seeing her example, other children were inspired to share their food with their poorer classmates. After that, no student in Amma's class had to go without food.

Once, when the teacher asked the students to write something, Amma noticed one girl weeping. On inquiry, Amma learnt that she did not have a pencil. Amma's pencil was only a little stub. Looking around, she noticed that one of the girls had a big pencil. In a twinkling, Amma grabbed it, broke it into two pieces, and gave one piece to the weeping girl. Unfortunately, this act of compassion was misunderstood by the teacher, who caned Amma for her mischief. Amma had not been acting for herself. Her innate compassion and selflessness were just manifesting themselves.

In the old days, not everyone had matchsticks at home, and it was not uncommon for those without them to go to a neighboring home where the cooking fire was lit to light their own firewood from the fire there. Whenever Amma went for this purpose or to collect food scraps, to be used as cattle-feed, she would help the elderly in those homes by doing their household chores. In this way, Amma became the uncrowned queen of everyone's hearts.

Just as Lord Krishna sheltered all of Vrindavan under the Govardhan Mountain during the seven-day deluge, Amma sheltered both the ashram residents and the villagers during the 2004 tsunami. She coordinated the immediate shifting of every villager from the peninsula to the mainland across the backwaters. Turning the university building into a relief camp, she arranged for their food, shelter, clothing and medical needs. Amma even gave personal swimming lessons to the village children to help them overcome their fear of water.

Amma's response to crises has not been confined to her village. She also initiated comprehensive relief and rehabilitation programs in the regions of Tamil Nadu and Sri Lanka affected by the 2004 tsunami. Similarly, the ashram also helped in the aftermath of the earthquake that struck Gujarat in 2001, Hurricane Katrina which hit the USA in 2005, the 2013 typhoon in the Philippines, the earthquake in Nepal in 2015, and so on.

Amma's care and concern are not limited to human beings alone but flow towards all of creation. In his book *'Color of the Rainbow,'* Swami Amritaswarupananda recounts a telling incident. A book chronicling all the relief activities that Amma had undertaken after the tsunami had been prepared. Before it was printed, Swamiji brought the mock-up to Amma for her approval. It contained photographs of volunteers—who included ashram residents of all age groups as well as Indian and Western devotees—participating enthusiastically in the relief work. There was also a photo of Ram, the ashram elephant, carrying a tree trunk to be used in building houses. Seeing this, Amma asked, "Where is Lakshmi? She was also doing *seva* (selfless service) alongside Ram!" Lakshmi is the other ashram elephant. Most of us might have regarded it as just a picture of an elephant, but for Amma, it was as if an important dignitary had been omitted! Nothing and no one are insignificant for her.

The ability to make good and timely decisions is also the hallmark of a leader. Once she has decided upon a course of action, Amma proves to be firm and fearless. During the 2002 riots in Gujarat, Amma's devotees in Mumbai and Gujarat pleaded with her not to go to Gujarat as part of her North Indian Tour. Amma heard everyone out, and then announced her decision: "I will go. Anybody who is afraid of death need not come." No one had to inculcate these qualities in Amma; she manifested them spontaneously when the need arose.

Wasn't Lord Krishna also like this? He was not afraid of anything. The deadly serpent Kaliya, which resided in the Kalindi, had polluted the river with its venom, and was keeping birds, beasts and human beings away. When Krishna heard about it, he dived right into the river, even though Mother Yashoda and others pleaded with him not to do so. He sprang onto Kaliya's head and began pounding the serpent's many hoods with his feet, causing it to vomit blood. It finally admitted defeat, promised the Lord that it would stop tormenting others, and left the river.

Amma walks her talk before she instructs anyone. During the COVID-19 pandemic, Amma herself began wearing a mask, thus inspiring her children to do so also. This is true of any work that she undertakes. Whether it is cleaning toilets, carrying loads of bricks, or stitching clothes for disaster victims, Amma is always the first person to start the work. Her humility is her greatness. Amma says, "I would like to be a sweeper, both of the inside and the outside."

There is a beautiful Malayalam song that describes a day of Sri Guruvayurappa, a form of Lord Krishna that is enshrined in the

Guruvayur Temple, Kerala. The poet describes how busy the Lord gets, answering prayers, healing his devotees, checking the temple accounts, and finally ending the day by attending *Krishnattam*, a traditional dance drama dedicated to him. By then, another day has dawned and his routine starts all over again!

It is the same with Amma. She does not have a single free minute to herself. As a conscientious mother, Amma has to wake her ashram children up in time for the morning archana. She has to ensure that they go for their morning walk, after which she has to send them off to scripture class and meditation. Soon after that, she has to come out for the public darshan program. By the time she has finished seeing and consoling the thousands of people who come for darshan, it is past midnight. After returning to her room, Amma settles down to read the many letters she receives from her children across the globe. Then she attends to institutional matters, makes phone calls and answers questions. After this, she checks the accounts of the various ashram institutions. If any ashram resident receives a call from Amma in the wee hours of the morning, it is probably because she has spotted some mistake in the balance sheet. In this way, Amma gives every minute of her time to the world. She is not interested in being anyone's leader, and considers herself the servant of servants. It is this humility and dedication to serving others that make her the truest leader.

# GLOSSARY

*abhisheka:* ceremonial bath, usually given to deities in a temple.

*Acchan:* Malayalam word for 'father.'

*adharma:* unrighteousness; deviation from natural harmony.

**Adi Shankaracharya:** saint revered as a Guru and chief proponent of the Advaita (non-dual) philosophy.

**Advaita:** not two; non-dual; philosophy that holds that the *jiva* (individual soul) and *jagat* (universe) are essentially one with *Brahman*, the supreme reality.

**AIMS:** Amrita Institute of Medical Sciences, a super-specialty hospital in Kochi, Kerala.

**Amma(chi)**: Malayalam word for 'mother.'

**Amrita Vidyalayam:** a national network of schools managed by the Mata Amritanandamayi Math and offering value-based education at the primary and secondary levels.

**Amrita Vishwa Vidyapeetham:** a private, deemed, multi-campus, multidisciplinary university, currently ranked among the best in India.

*arati:* clockwise movement of a lamp aflame with burning camphor, to propitiate a deity, usually signifying the closing of a ceremonial worship.

*archana:* chanting of the 108 or 1,000 names of a particular deity (e.g. *'Lalita Sahasranama'*).

*artha:* goal, wealth, substance; one of the four *purusharthas* (goals of human endeavor).

*asana:* physical posture, usually referring to yoga postures or sitting postures during meditation. Also, the seat on which one sits for spiritual practice.

*ashram:* monastery. Amma defines it as a compound: *'a'* — 'that' and *'shramam'* — 'effort' (toward Self-realization).

*Ashtottaram:* litany of 108 attributes of a deity, divine incarnation or saint; short form of *ashtottara-shatam* (108) or *ashtottara-shata-namavali* (108 names).

*atma*: Self or soul.

**avatar:** from Sanskrit root *'ava–tarati'* — 'to come down.' Divine incarnation.

**AYUDH:** 'Amrita Yuva Dharmadhara,' the youth wing of the Mata Amritanandamayi Math.

*Bhagavad Gita:* 'Song of the Lord,' it consists of 18 chapters of verses in which Lord Krishna advises Arjuna. The advice is given on the battlefield of Kurukshetra, just before the righteous Pandavas fight the unrighteous Kauravas. It is a practical guide to overcoming crises in one's personal or social life and is the essence of Vedic wisdom.

*bhajan:* devotional song or hymn in praise of God.

*bhakta:* devotee.

*bhakti:* devotion for God.

*bhava:* divine mood or attitude.

*bhava darshan:* see darshan.

*bhaya-bhakti:* devotion arising from fear of repercussion.

*brahmachari:* celibate male disciple who practices spiritual disciplines under a Guru's guidance; *'brahmacharini'* is the female equivalent.

***Brahman:*** ultimate truth beyond any attributes; the supreme reality underlying all life; the divine ground of existence.

***Brahmasthanam:*** 'abode of Brahman.' The name of the temples Amma consecrated in various parts of India and in Mauritius. The temple shrine features a unique four-faced idol that symbolizes the unity behind the diversity of divine forms.

**Brahmin:** member of the priestly caste.

*darshan:* audience with a holy person or a vision of the Divine. Amma's signature darshan is a hug.

**Devi:** Goddess / Divine Mother.

***Devi Bhagavatam:*** also known as *Devi Bhagavata Purana*, a Sanskrit composition that narrates the life, pastimes and teachings of various manifestations of Devi.

***Devi Bhava:*** 'the divine mood of Devi;' occasion when Amma reveals her oneness with the Divine Mother.

*dharma:* 'that which upholds (creation).' Generally refers to the harmony of the universe, a righteous code of conduct, sacred duty or eternal law.

*dhyana shloka:* benedictory verse.

*diksha:* initiation into the vows of *brahmacharya* or *sannyasa* or any form of spiritual discipline such as *japa* (repeated chanting of a mantra) and *dhyana* (meditation).

*dvesha:* aversion.

*gopa:* cowherd boy from Vrindavan.

*gopi:* milk maiden from Vrindavan. The gopis were known for their ardent devotion to Lord Krishna. Their devotion exemplifies the most intense love for God.

***grhasta:*** householder; member of the second of four *ashramas* (stages of life), which include *brahmacharya* (celibate student life), *garhasthya* (married householder life), *vanaprastha* (life of retirement and contemplation) and *sannyasa*.

**Guru:** spiritual teacher.

***gurukula:*** literally, the clan (*kula*) of the preceptor (*Guru*); traditional school where students would stay with the Guru for the entire duration of their scriptural studies.

***Hari-katha:*** literally, 'story of Hari (Lord Vishnu);' a traditional form of discourse in which the narration is interspersed with singing.

**IAM™:** Integrated Amrita Meditation,™ a meditation practice formulated by Amma, one that synthesizes simple yoga, *pranayama* (breathing) and concentration techniques.

***jivan mukti:*** spiritual liberation while alive.

***jnana:*** knowledge of the Truth. A *jnani* is one who knows the Truth.

***kalari:*** generally, a center for martial arts training; here, it refers to a temple where Amma used to hold Krishna Bhava and Devi Bhava darshans.

**Kali:** Goddess of fearsome aspect; depicted as dark, wearing a garland of skulls, and a girdle of human hands; feminine of Kala (time).

***kama:*** desire.

***kanji:*** rice gruel.

***karma:*** action; mental, verbal and physical activity; chain of effects produced by our actions.
***karma kushalata:*** skill or dexterity in action.
***karma yoga:*** the way of action, the path of selfless service.
**Kauravas:** the 101 children of King Dhritarashtra and Queen Gandhari, of whom the unrighteous Duryodhana was the eldest. The Kauravas were the enemies of their cousins, the virtuous Pandavas, whom they fought against in the Mahabharata War.
**Krishna:** from '*krish,*' meaning 'to draw to oneself' or 'to remove sin;' principal incarnation of Lord Vishnu. He was born into a royal family but raised by foster parents, and lived as a cowherd boy in Vrindavan, where he was loved and worshipped by his devoted companions, the *gopis* (milkmaids) and *gopas* (cowherd boys). Krishna later established the city of Dvaraka. He was a friend and advisor to his cousins, the Pandavas, especially Arjuna, whom he served as charioteer during the Mahabharata War, and to whom he revealed his teachings as the *Bhagavad Gita*.
**Krishna Bhava:** 'the divine mood of Krishna,' occasion when Amma reveals her oneness with Lord Krishna.

***Lalita Sahasranama:*** litany of 1,000 names of Sri Lalita Devi, a form of the Goddess.
***lila:*** divine play.

**Ma-Om meditation:** a meditation technique formulated by Amma, one that involves synchronizing the silent intonation of the syllables 'Ma' and 'Om' with the inhalation and exhalation.

*Mahabharata:* ancient Indian epic that Sage Vyasa composed, depicting the war between the righteous Pandavas and the unrighteous Kauravas.

*maharishi:* 'great rishi;' see rishi.

*mahatma:* 'great soul;' term used to describe one who has attained spiritual realization.

*manasa puja:* worship done mentally.

*mantra:* a sound, syllable, word or words of spiritual content. According to Vedic commentators, mantras are revelations of rishis arising from deep contemplation.

*Matruvani:* 'Voice of the Mother.' The ashram's flagship publication dedicated to disseminating Amma's teachings and chronicling her divine mission. It is currently published in 17 languages (including nine Indian languages).

**Maya:** cosmic delusion, personified as a temptress. Illusion; appearance, as contrasted with reality; the creative power of the Lord; see Shakti.

*mithya:* changing, therefore impermanent. Also, illusory or untrue. According to Vedanta, the entire visible world is mithya.

*moksha:* spiritual liberation, i.e. release from the cycle of births and deaths.

*mudra:* hand gesture of mystical import.

*nirguna:* without attributes (as opposed to saguna).

**Om (Aum):** primordial sound in the universe; the seed of creation. The cosmic sound, which can be heard in deep meditation; the Holy Word, taught in the Upanishads, which signifies Brahman, the divine ground of existence.

**Onam:** Kerala's biggest festival, occurring in the month of *Chingam* (August – September).

*paapa:* sin; wrongdoing.

*pancabhuta:* The five (*panca*) elements (*bhutas*) that are the material cause of creation. The five elements are *akash* (ether), *vayu* (air), *agni* (fire), *jalam* (water) and *prthvi* (earth).

**Pandavas:** five sons of King Pandu, and cousins of Krishna.

**Parashakti:** supreme power, personified as the Goddess or Empress of the Universe.

*payasam:* sweet pudding.

*prana:* vital force.

*prarabdha:* also known as *prarabdha karma*. It refers to the portion of our past karma that is the cause of our present birth.

*prasad:* blessed offering or gift from a holy person or temple, often in the form of food.

*pratishtha:* the installation and consecration of an idol in a temple.

*puja:* ritualistic or ceremonial worship.

*punya:* spiritual merit.

**Puranas:** compendium of stories, including the biographies and stories of gods, saints, kings and great people; allegories and chronicles of great historical events that aim to make the teachings of the Vedas simple and available to all.

*purna:* full or whole; spiritual fullness.

*raga:* attachment.

**Rama:** divine hero of the *Ramayana*. An incarnation of Lord Vishnu, he is considered the ideal man of *dharma* and virtue. 'Ram' means 'to revel;' one who revels in himself; the principle of joy within; one who gladdens the hearts of others.

**Ramakrishna Paramahamsa:** spiritual master (1836 – 1886) from West Bengal, hailed as the apostle of religious harmony. He generated a spiritual renaissance that continues to touch the lives of millions.

**Ramana Maharshi:** spiritual master (1879 – 1950) who lived in Tiruvannamalai, Tamil Nadu. He recommended Self-inquiry as the path to Liberation, though he approved of a variety of paths and spiritual practices.

*Ramayana:* 24,000-verse epic poem on the life and times of Rama.

*rishi:* spiritually enlightened being and seer to whom mantras and the secrets of the universe were revealed in deep meditation.

*sadhana:* regimen of disciplined and dedicated spiritual practice that leads to the supreme goal of Self-realization.

*sahaja samadhi: samadhi* that is constant and natural.

*samadhi:* literally, 'cessation of all mental movements;' oneness with God; a transcendental state in which one loses all sense of individual identity; union with absolute reality; a state of intense concentration in which consciousness is completely unified.

*samatva:* even-mindedness or equanimity.

*samsara:* cycle of births and deaths; the world of flux; the wheel of birth, decay, death and rebirth.

**Sanatana Dharma:** literally, 'Eternal Religion' or 'Eternal Way of Life,' the original and traditional name of Hinduism.

*sankalpa:* divine resolve, usually used in association with *mahatmas*.

*sannyasi:* monk who has taken formal vows of renunciation (*sannyasa*); traditionally wears an ocher-colored robe, representing the burning away of all desires. The female equivalent is *sannyasini*.

**Sanskrit:** language of the oldest sacred text, the *Rk Veda*, and the other three Vedas; the language of most ancient Hindu scriptures.

**Sarada Devi:** spiritual master (1853 – 1920) and consort of Sri Ramakrishna Paramahamsa whom devotees of Sri Ramakrishna reverentially addressed as the Holy Mother.

*sat-cit-ananda:* literally, 'existence-consciousness-bliss,' a description of the subjective experience of the Supreme.

**Satguru:** 'true master.' All Satgurus are *mahatmas*, but not all mahatmas are Satgurus. The Satguru is one who, while still experiencing the bliss of the Self, chooses to come down to the level of ordinary people to help them grow spiritually.

*satsang:* communion with the Supreme Truth. Also, being in the company of *mahatmas*, studying the scriptures, and listening to the enlightening talks of a mahatma; a meeting of people to listen to and/or discuss spiritual matters; a spiritual discourse.

*seva:* selfless service, the results of which are dedicated to God.

**Shakti:** personification of cosmic will and energy; strength.

**Shiva:** worshipped as the first and the foremost in the lineage of Gurus, and as the formless substratum of the universe in relationship to Shakti. The Lord of Destruction in the Hindu Trinity.

*shraddha:* attentiveness; faith.

***Srimad Bhagavatam:*** also known as *Bhagavatam*, a Sanskrit composition that upholds devotion to Lord Vishnu, the Creator in the Hindu Trinity. It is one of the 18 *Puranas*. It narrates the life, pastimes and teachings of various incarnations of Vishnu, chiefly that of Lord Krishna.

*sthita-prajna:* person of 'steady wisdom,' who has renounced all desires and is established in the Self.

**swami, swamini:** title of one who has taken the vow of *sannyasa* (see *sannyasi*); swamini is the female equivalent.

**Swami Vivekananda:** chief disciple (1863 – 1902) of Sri Ramakrishna Paramahamsa, a pioneer in introducing Hindu philosophy to the West, and founder of the Ramakrishna Math and Ramakrishna Mission.

*tabla:* a pair of Indian hand drums.
*tapas:* austerities, penance.

**Upanishad:** portions of the Vedas dealing with Self-knowledge.

**Valmiki:** sage and author of the *Ramayana*.
*vasana:* latent tendency or subtle desire that manifests as thought, motive and action; subconscious impression gained from experience.
**Vedas:** most ancient of all scriptures, originating from God, the Vedas were not composed by any human author but were 'revealed' in deep meditation to the ancient seers. These sagely revelations came to be known as the Vedas, of which there are four: *Rk*, *Yajus*, *Sama* and *Atharva*.
**Vedanta:** 'the end of the Vedas.' It refers to the Upanishads, which deal with the subject of Brahman, the supreme truth, and the path to realize that Truth; a Vedantin is a follower of Vedanta.
**Vishnu:** Lord of Sustenance in the Hindu Trinity.

***Vishu:*** popular Hindu festival celebrated in Kerala and which coincides with the spring equinox.

***vishvas:*** faith.

***viveka:*** discernment, especially between the ephemeral and eternal.

**White Flower meditation:** a meditation technique formulated by Amma in which the practitioner visualizes the showering of white flowers of peace falling all over the earth; a visualization technique aimed at fostering peace in human hearts.

***yajna:*** form of ritual worship in which oblations are offered into a fire according to scriptural injunctions, while sacred mantras are chanted.

***yoga:*** 'to unite.' Union with the Supreme Being. A broad term, it also refers to the various methods of practices through which one can attain oneness with the Divine. A path that leads to Self-realization.

***yogi:*** a practitioner or an adept of yoga; ***yogini*** is the female equivalent.

**Yudhishthira:** the eldest of the righteous Pandava brothers who waged war against the Kauravas, their unrighteous cousins, in the *Mahabharata*.

***yuga:*** according to Hindu cosmogony, the universe (from origin to dissolution) passes through a cycle made up of four Yugas or ages. The first is *Krta Yuga*, during which dharma reigns in society. Each succeeding age sees the progressive decline of dharma. The second age is known as *Treta Yuga*, the third is *Dvapara Yuga*, and the fourth and present epoch is known as *Kali Yuga*.

Printed in the USA
CPSIA information can be obtained
at www.ICGtesting.com
CBHW081637070624
9541CB00007B/7